AN EMPIRICAL STUDY ON ORGANISATIONAL CLIMATE AND JOB SATISFACTION IN TTD

Thesis submitted to

SRI VENKATESWARA UNIVERSITY

For the award of the degree of

DOCTOR OF PHILOSOPHY

IN

COMMERCE

By

Mr. C. BRAHMAIAH

Under the supervision of

Prof. M. VENKATESWARLU,

M.Com., M.Phil., Ph.D.,

DEPARTMENT OF COMMERCE
SRI VENKATESWARA UNIVERSITY
TIRUPATI-517 502, A. P. INDIA

DECEMBER 2010

Declaration

I hereby declare that the research work presented in the thesis entitled **"AN EMPIRICAL STUDY ON ORGANISATIONAL CLIMATE AND JOB SATISFACTION IN TTD"** submitted by me in partial fulfillment of the requirements for the award of the Degree of Doctor of Philosophy in Commerce of Sri Venkateswara University, Tirupati. I further declare that the thesis is a result of own effort has not been submitted to any other university for the award of any degree of diploma.

Place: Tirupati
Date:

(C. BRAHMAIAH)

Prof.
M.Venkateswarlu

M.com., M.Phil., Ph.D.,
Department of Commerce
S.V.U. College of Commerce,
Management &Computer science,
S.V.University,

Phone Off. 0877-2289461
Res.0877- 2248501

Date: 31 - 12 - 2010

Certificate

This is to certify that the thesis entitled "AN EMPIRICAL STUDY ON ORGANISATIONAL CLIMATE AND JOB SATISFACTION IN TTD" submitted to Sri Venkateswara University by **Mr. C. BRAHMAIAH** for the award of the Degree of Doctor of Philosophy in Commerce is a bonafide record of research work carried out by him under my guidance and supervision and has not been submitted to any other University or Institution for the award of any Degree or Diploma.

(Prof. M. VENKATESWARLU)
Research Supervisor

Acknowledgements

It is my pleasant duty to acknowledge the help, assistance and co-operation I have received from many persons, institutions and organizations at different stages of this work.

I sincerely express my indebtedness and deep sense of gratitude to my research supervisor **Prof. M.VENKATESWARLU**, Department of Commerce, Sri Venkateswara University, Tirupati, for his constant help, unstinted support and inspiring guidance throughout the period of this work.

I take this opportunity to express my gratitude to **Prof. T. Siddaiah**, Dean and Principal, **Prof. B.Mohan**, **Prof. K. Ramakrishnaiah**, Head of the Department, **Prof. D. Himachalam**, Chairman and B.O.S., **Prof. B.Bhagavan Reddy, Prof. K.Jayachadra, Prof. M. Rajasekhar, Prof. P.Mohan Reddy, Prof. B.Ramachandra Reddy, Prof. P.V. Narasaiah,** faculty Members of Department of Commerce, Sri Venkateswara University, Tirupati, for their kind co-operation and encouragement.

I express my deep sense of gratitude to **Prof. P. Bala Siddamuni**, Professor of Statistics, Sri Venkateswara University, Tirupati, for his invaluable help, guidance and suggestions in statistical methods and analysis.

I wish to express my gratitude to the Management of the TTD, for providing necessary information and according permission for collecting the primary and secondary data related to my study. I owe much to the sample respondents of the TTD for having responded to the structure questionnaire canvassed to them.

I am thankful to the authorities of Sri Venkateswara University, Tirupati for providing me the research facilities and to the Librarian and other staff of Sri Venkateswara University Library, Tirupati for placing at my disposal the necessary books, journals.

I sincerely thank my fellow- research scholars and friends **Dr. Ravi Prasad, Dr. G. Tirumalaiah, Mr. Ramalingaiah, Mr. M. Sankar Nayak,** for their constant help, co-operation and encouragement.

I extend my sincere thanks last but not least to **Mr. P. Indramuni** and **S.Pradeep Kumar, Indra Xerox** for their timely typing the manuscript and giving the typed material on time.

I could like to express my grateful acknowledgements to writers whose contributions are quoted in the study as well as in the Bibliography.

This is a long list and there must have been many others. I am thankful to all of them.

(C. BRAHMAIAH)

CONTENTS

Chapter - I

A THEORETICAL FRAME WORK OF ORGANISATIONAL CLIMATE AND JOB SATISFACTION

Climate for an organization is like personality for a person. "Just as every individual has a personality that makes each person unique, each organization has an organizational climate that clearly distinguishes its personality from other organizations".[1] The concept of organizational climate was formalised by the human relation theorists in the late 1940s. Now it has become a very useful metaphor for thinking about and describing the social system. Organizational climate is also referred to as the "situational determinants" or "environmental determinants" which affect the human behaviour. Some persons have used organizational culture and organizational climate interchangeably. But there are some basic differences between these two terms. According to Bowditch and Buono, "organizational culture is connected with the nature of beliefs and expectations about organizational life, while climate is an indicator of whether these beliefs and expectations are being fulfilled".

According to Joe Kelly, "climate may be thought of as the perception of the characteristics of an organization."[2] Organisational climate conveys the impressions of people regarding organizational internal environment within which they work. It may also be viewed as the degree to which organizational rules are enforced by the administrative component. It may refer to the extent to which persons are treated as "human beings" rather than as "cogs" in machine.

"Organizational climate is the summary perception, which people have about an organisation. It is a global expression of what the organisation is."[3] Organisational climate is the manifestation of the attitudes of organizational members toward the organisation itself. An organisation tends to attract and keep people who fit in its climate, so that its patterns are perpetuated at least to some extent.

When considered collectively, the actions of the individual become more meaningful for the total impact upon the climate and determining the stability of the work environment. It should be noted that the climate is to be viewed from a total system perspective. While there may be differences in climate within sub system (departments), these will be integrated to a certain extent to denote overall organizational climate.

Organizational climate is the root cause of the success or failure of every organization. It is the resultant effect of an interaction of a number of internal variables like structure, system, culture, leaders' behaviour, working conditions and psychological needs of employees with one another. Organizational climate is generally perceived or felt by the employees. More often than not, by the term, organizational climate, we mean, perceived climate. Organizational climate represents the entire social system of a work group. Two important aspects of climate are the work place and the treatment received from management. Employees feel that the climate is favorable when they are doing something useful that provides a sense of personal worth.

Employees expect certain rewards and satisfaction or feel frustrated, based upon their perception of the organization's climate. These expectations tend to lead to motivation as explained by expectancy theory. Climate exists in a contingency relationship with the organization. It means that the type of climate that an organization seeks is contingent on the type of employees it has, the type of technology, the education of workers, and similar variables.

Organizational climate is a very important factor to be considered in studying and analyzing organizations because it has a profound influence on the outlook, well – being and attitudes of organizational members and, thus, on their total performance.

Concept of organizational climate

"Climate in a natural sense is referred to as the average course or condition of the weather at a place over a period of years as exhibited by temperature, wind, velocity and precipitation."

However, it is quite difficult to define organizational climate incorporating the characteristics of natural climate. This is so because the most frustrating feature of an attempt to deal with situational variables in a model of management performance is the enormous complexity of the management itself. People have defined organizational climate on the basis of its potential properties. A few important definitions are as given below.

According to Forehand and Gilmer (1964) [4] "Climate consists of a set of characteristics that describe an organization and that: (a) distinguish one organisation from other organizations (b) are relatively enduring over a period of time, and (c) influence the behaviour of people in the organisation."

According to Litwin and Stringer (1968) [5] "Organizational Climate refers to the perceived, subjective effect of the formal system, the formal 'style' of managers, and other important environmental factors on the attitudes, beliefs, values and motivation of people who work in a particular organization."

According to Campbell et al. (1970) [6] "Organizational climate can be defined as a set of attributes specific to a particular organization that may be induced from the way that organization deals with its members and its environment. For the individual members with the organization, climate takes the form of a set of attitudes and experiences which describe the organization in terms of both static characteristics (such as degree of autonomy) and behaviour outcomes and outcome-outcome contingencies."

Baumgartel (1971) [7] says 'Organisational climate is a product of leadership practice, communication patterns, enduring and systematic characteristics of the working relationship among persons and divisions of any particular organisation'.

According to this definition, organizational climate may be regarded as the 'personality' of an organization as perceived by its employees. The totality of personality of individuals working in the organization has an impact on it and also the climate that emerges within an organization represents a major determinant of employees' behaviour.

Thus, organizational climate is a relatively enduring quality of the internal environment that is experienced by its members, influences their behaviour and can be described in terms of the value of a particular set of characteristics of the organization. It may be possible to have as many climates as there are people in the organization. When considered collectively, the actions of the individuals become more meaningful for viewing the total impact upon the climate and determining the

4

stability of the work environment. The climate should be viewed from a total system perspective. While there may be differences in climates within departments, these will be integrated to a certain extent to denote overall organizational climate.

FACTORS INFLUENCING ORGANIZATIONAL CLIMATE

Organizational climate is a manifestation of the attitudes of organizational members towards the organization. In every organization there exist certain elements that exert profound influence on the existing climate. The researcher has used the data relating to individual perception of organizational properties in identifying organizational climate. Even in this context, there is a great amount of diversity.

Garlise A. Forehand and B. Von Haller Gilmer (1964)[8]: Established the following five dimensions.

a. Size: Deals with the position of the individual in the organization

b. Structure: Deals with structure of authority and relationships among persons and groups.

c. System of complexity: Deals with the number of components and number and nature of interactions among the systems employed by the organization.

d. Leadership style: Deals with the personality measure of individuals in leadership positions.

e. Goal Direction: Deals with organizational goals and the relative weight placed on main and subsidiary goals.

Litwin and Stringer (1966)[9]: Have included six factors, which affect of organizational climate. These factors are:

1. Organizational Structure – perceptions of the extent of organizational constraints, rules, regulations, red tape;

2. Individual Responsibility – feeling of autonomy, of being one's own boss;

3. Rewards – feelings related to being confident of adequate and appropriate rewards;

4. Risk and Risk Taking – perceptions of the degree of challenge and risk in the work situation;

5. Warmth and Support – feeling of general good fellowship and helpfulness prevailing in the work setting; and

6. Tolerance and Conflict – degree of confidence that the climate can tolerate, differing opinions.

Likert (1967)[10]: Proposed six dimensions of organizational climate: leadership, motivation, communication, decisions, goals and control.

A broader and somewhat more systematic study of climate dimensions described by **Schneider and Bartlett (1968)** [11]: include six items that are important in determining organizational climate. These are

(a) Management Support.

(b) Management Structure.

(c) Concern for new employees

(d) Inter – agency conflict.

(e) Agent dependence, and

(f) General Satisfaction

Taguiri (1970) [12]: Has identified five factors influencing the organizational climate on the basis of information provided by managers. These are:

(a) Practices relating to providing a sense of direction or purpose to their jobs – setting of objectives, planning and feedback;

(b) Opportunities for exercising individual initiative;

(c) Working with a superior who is highly competitive and competent;

(d) Working with cooperative and pleasant people; and

(e) Being with a profit oriented and sales oriented company.

Robert D. Pritchard and Bernard W. Karasick (1973) [13]: Measured organizational climate using 11 dimensions.

(1) Autonomy: degree of freedom managers have in day-to-day operating decisions such as when to work, when not to work, and how to solve job problems.

(2) Conflict vs. cooperation: degree to which managers either compete with each other or work together in getting things done and in the allocation of scarce resources such as material, clerical help, etc.

(3) Social relations: degree to which the organization has a friendly and warm social atmosphere.

(4) Structure: degree to which the organization specifies the methods and procedures used to accomplish tasks; the degree to which the organization likes to specify and codify, and write things down in a very explicit form.

(5) Level of rewards: degree or extent to which managers are well rewarded; this includes salary, fringe benefits, and other status symbols.

(6) Performance- reward dependency: extent to which the reward system (salary, promotion, benefits, etc.) is fair and appropriate; degree to which these rewards are based on worth, ability, and past performance rather than factors such as luck, how well a manager can manipulate people, etc.

(7) Motivation to achieve: degree to which the organization attempts to excel; the strength of its desire to be number one. A high rating reflects a lack of complacency even in the face of good profits, etc.

(8) Status polarization: degree to which there are definite physical distinctions (e.g., special parking places and office decorations) as well as psychological distinctions (informal social boundaries, treatment of the subordinate as inferior, etc.,) between managerial levels in the organization.

(9) Flexibility of innovation: willingness to try new procedures and experiment with change which is not really necessary due to some potential crisis situations, but rather to improve a situation or process which may currently be working satisfactorily.

(10) Decision centralization: extent to which the organization delegates the responsibility for making decisions either as widely as possible or centralizes it as much as possible. Decentralization includes the idea of shared decision making.

(11) Supportiveness: degree to which the organization is interested in and is willing to support its managers in both job-and non-job-related matters.

Lawrence James and Allan Jones (1974) [14]: Have classified the following factors that influence organizational climate into five major components;

(a) Organizational context – mission, goals and objectives, function, etc.

(b) Organizational structure – size, degree of centralization and operating procedures.

(c) Leadership process – leadership styles, communication, decision-making and related processes.

(d) Physical environment – employee safety, environmental stresses and physical space characteristics.

(e) Organizational values and norms – conformity, loyalty, impersonality and reciprocity.

According to John E.Newman (1977) [15] the 11 empirical- derived dimensions of perceived work environment are;

(1) Supervisory style- the extent to which the supervisor is open, supportive and considerate.

(2) Task characteristics – the extent to which the jobs /tasks are characterized by variety, challenge, worthwhile accomplishment, etc.

(3) Performance –Reward relationships- – the extent to which rewards such as promotions and salary increases are based on performance rather than on other consideration such as favoritism.

(4) Co-worker Relations – the extent to which co-workers are trustworthy, supporting, friendly and cooperative.

(5) Employee work Motivation – the extent to which employees show concern for the quality of their work, try to get ahead, are involved in their work, etc.

(6) Equipment and Arrangement of People and Equipment – the extent to which the equipment and arrangement of people and equipment allow for efficient and effective work operations.

(7) Employee competence – the extent to which the employees have the proper background, training and "know-how" to do what is expected of them.

(8) Decision making policy– the extent to which employees take part in decisions that affect their work situation.

(9) Work space – the extent to which employees have adequate work space and freedom to move.

(10) Pressure to produce – the extent to which there are pressures to produce

(11) Job responsibility / importance– the extent to which employees see responsibility as part of their job and the work as necessary to the successful operation of the organization.

Pareek (1987)[16]: Has defined the framework for motivational analysis of organizational climate (MAO-C) around twelve dimensions and six motives.

Orientation, interpersonal relationship, supervision, problem management, management of mistakes, conflict management, communication, decision making, trust, management rewards, risk taking, innovation and change.

Motives of organizational climate – Achievement, Expert influence, Control, Dependency, Extension and Affiliation.

Richard M. Hodgetts (1991) [17]: Has classified organizational climate into two major categories. He has given the analogy of the iceberg where there is a part of the iceberg that can be seen from the surface and another part that is under the water and cannot be seen. The factors in the visible part that can be observed and measured are called overt factors and the factors that are not visible and quantifiable are called covert factors. Both these factors are shown in the following paragraph.

Overt Factors- Hierarchy, Financial Resources, Goals of Organization, Skills and Abilities of Personnel, Technological State, Performance Standards, and Efficiency Measurement.

Covert Factors – Attitudes, Feelings, Value, Norms, Interaction, Supportiveness, and Satisfaction.

The above dimensions or components which collectively represent the climate of an organization are as discussed below: The results of the studies show that it is very difficult to generalize the basic contents of organizational climate but based on these studies, it becomes clear that it is a multi-dimensional concept. However, some broad generalizations can be drawn and it can be concluded that four basic factors are somewhat common to the findings of most studies. These factors are:

(a) Individual autonomy

(b) The degree of structure imposed upon the position.

(c) Reward Orientation

(d) Consideration, warmth and support.

Another common factor can be in respect of conflict and cooperation. But different people view this factor in different ways.

DIMENSIONS OF ORGANISATIONAL CLIMATE FOR THE PRESENT STUDY

A questionnaire with statements was developed to measure the employee perceptions of the climate based on the determinants of climate identified by some earlier researchers such as Blades R. Sharma (1987), Shailendra Singh (1988), and Uthayasuriyan, (1989). The structured questionnaire was revised on the basis of a pre-tested questionnaire which was administered TTD employees group in Tirumala Tiruapti Devasthanams, which included Professionals, Administrative staff, and Sub-staff. The revised structured questionnaire contained 79 statements grouped under the following 19 dimensions.

1. Managerial Structure and Policies- interest in and evaluation of ideas from subordinates by the management; constraints felt by the employees; quick and accurate decision-making; degree to which the leader is open, supportive and considerate.

2. Recognition and Appreciation- recognition and appreciation of sincere and hard working employees and of those contributing to the productivity and efficiency of the organization.

3. Participative Management- involvement of employees in solving day-to-day problems; competency and effective performance of various committees; recognition given to workers' representative in meetings; negotiation in decision-making.

4. Supervision- supervisory practices contribute significantly to climate and atmosphere. If supervisors focus on helping their subordinates to improve personal skills and chances of advancement, a climate that is characterized by the extension motive may result. If supervisors are more concerned with maintaining good relations with their subordinates, a climate characterized by the affiliation motive may result.

5. Conflict Avoidance- In the organization, there can always be inter-group as well as intra-group conflicts. The organizational climate will depend upon how effectively these conflicts are managed. If they are managed effectively, there will be an atmosphere of cooperation in the organization. If they are not managed properly, there will be an atmosphere of distrust and non-cooperation.

When the workers are powerful, they may resort to conflict to change the organizational climate in their favour. If the workers fail in their attempt, there will be hostility and lack of trust in their relationships with the management. Thus, conflict may prove detrimental to the organizational climate. The management should try to create an environment wherein conflicts can be controlled. Whenever genuine conflicts arise, they should be settled to the satisfaction of both the parties. 'win-win' strategy is likely to improve the organizational climate.

6. Warmth- relaxed and easy going working climate; lot of warmth in the relationship between management and employees; a friendly atmosphere prevails among the employees.

7. Social Values- consideration given to the social needs of the members; status of the job in society; feeling of prestige; chance of moving with the public.

8. Training and Advancement- provision of adequate facilities for general education and technical training to the employees; adequate opportunities for advancement and growth, existence of definite career development plans for employees.

9. Grievance Handling- existence of sound grievance handling procedure; readiness of the management to look into the grievances and complaints of employees.

10. Individual Autonomy- by helping the individual to form a perception; organizational factors influence the behaviour by helping the individual in forming a perception of the organization. The perception then influences behaviour.

11. Individual Responsibility- always feel responsible at work; if at times things do not go well, I do take responsibility.

12. Performance Standards- very high Standards for performance; rules and regulations for handling any kind problems that are related to work are solved quickly; importance is given for high quality of work.

13. Mutual Trust- The degree of mutual trust or lack of trust among various members and groups in the organization affects the climate. If there is mutual trust between different individuals, groups and also between management and workers, there

will be peace in the organization. The members will cooperate with one another for the attainment of organizational objectives.

14. Awards and Rewards System- The system of awards and rewards is also an important component of organizational climate. If the reward system is directly related to performance and productivity, there will be an atmosphere of competition among the employees. Everybody will like to work hard and earn more rewards in the form of promotions and pay rise. If there is bias in the distribution of rewards, the meritorious employees will be discouraged.

15. Work Relation- towards peers, the management, union and others; a sense of belongingness to the organization.

16. Decision Making- decisions are made in consultation with the unions; mainly the experts are involved in the decision making process.

17. Welfare Facilities – provisions of safe and healthy working conditions; adequate job security; attractive retirement benefits, realistic and reasonable work standards, and adequate welfare facilities and amenities to employees at their work place and outside.

18. Communication- The communication system of the organization will also affect the organizational climate. The flow of information, its direction (top – down, bottom – up, horizontal), its disbursement (selectively or to everyone concerned), its mode (formal or informal), and its type are all important determinants. Proper communication system means that the subordinates are in a position to express their ideas, suggestions and reactions, otherwise they will feel frustrated.

19. Unions -   the formation and functioning of the unions; trade union leadership is acquired on democratic lines; issue for collective bargaining are determined in consultation with union members; Unions are effective in solving problems of the employees; union-management relations are cordial.

JOB SATISFACTION

INTRODUCTION

Job satisfaction is the employee's general attitude towards his job, management and the organization. A job provides both monetary benefits as well as satisfaction. Employees develop general attitude while they interact with each other, with the general public, customers, manager, and administration and also with the members of their societies. Employees may feel satisfied, moderately satisfied or highly satisfied. Similarly, they also develop negative attitudes on the satisfaction scale. Task varieties, significance and other characteristics are the important factors for providing satisfaction to the employees. Many employees are satisfied with complex jobs while others are satisfied with simple jobs. Thus, employees perceive jobs as satisfying or dissatisfying. Sometimes, the employee's perception may not be in consonance with reality. However, cognitive satisfaction is an important factor to understand employee's satisfaction with the job.

Meaning of Job Satisfaction

Employees Job satisfaction is of great significance for efficient and profitable functioning of an organization. Satisfied workforce is the greatest asset to any organization and dissatisfied employees are the biggest liability. In fact, no organization can successfully achieve its goals unless and until those who constitute the organization are satisfied in their jobs. It is believed that employees dissatisfied with their jobs may be militant in their attitudes towards the management.

Job satisfaction refers either to a person or a group. It results from the best fit among job requirement, wants and expectations of an employee. It is used to express the extent of match between the employees' expectations of the job and the rewards that the job provides. Job satisfaction is the result of various attitudes the person holds towards his job or towards life in general.

14

CONCEPT OF JOB SATISFACTION

The term job satisfaction came in vogue in 1935 with the publishing of a book "job satisfaction "by Hoppock. He was the first industrial psychologist who provided the concept of job satisfaction. **Hoppock (1935)** [18] defined job satisfaction as "any combination of psychological, physiological and environmental circumstances that causes a person truthfully to say, I am satisfied with the job".

In the words of **Bullock (1952)** [19] "job satisfaction is an attitude which results from balancing and summation of many specific likes and dislikes, feelings experienced by employees in connection with their job".

According to **Smith, H.C (1955)** [20] "job satisfaction is the employee's judgment of how well his job on the whole is satisfying his various needs".

Keith Davis (1977) [21] considered job satisfaction as "the favourableness or unfavourableness with which employees view their work. It results when there is a fit between job characteristics and wants of employees. It expresses the amount congruence between one's expectations of the job and the rewards that the job provides".

Pestonjee (1991) [22] defined job satisfaction as "summation of employees" feelings in four important areas, namely, job, management, personal adjustment and social relations. The first two areas encompass factors directly connected with the job (intrinsic factors) and the other two include factors not directly connected with job but which are presumed to have a bearing on job satisfaction (extrinsic factors)".

According to these definitions, job satisfaction can be perceived or imagined judgment of how well the job life is satisfying the various needs, accounts for the degree of job satisfaction and dissatisfaction. For perfect job satisfaction there should exist a one to one relationship between perception of how well the job's life fulfils the various needs and expectations or aspirations of the individual and the extent to which these needs are actually fulfilled. Job satisfaction is part of life satisfaction. The nature of one's job environment affects his satisfaction. Job satisfaction is, to a large extent, governed by perceptions and expectations.

THEORIES OF JOB SATISFACTION

Theories dealing with job satisfaction can be broadly divided into two theories; one, content theories and two, process theories.

1. Content theories – these theories made an attempt to identify the factors that lead to job satisfaction and motivate people to work. These include (i) Maslow's Theory of Need Hierarchy and (ii) Herzberg's Two Factor Theory

2. Process theories - process theories provided a much sounder theoretical explanation of work motivation and job satisfaction. These include: (i) Vroom's Expectancy Theory

1) Abraham H. Maslow's Theory of Need Hierarchy

According to the need hierarchy notion of Maslow (1943) [23] jobs, which are able to satisfy, more needs of the individual would be jobs that would result in greater satisfaction on the part of the employee. Maslow's theory is a clinically derived theory. He indicated five levels of needs as given below.

(a) Physiological Needs

Physiological needs are the biological needs required to preserve human life; these needs include needs for food, clothing and shelter. These needs must be met at least partly before higher level needs emerge. They exert a tremendous influence on behaviour. They are the most powerful of motivating stimuli; for we must satisfy most of them in order to exist (survive). These take precedence over other needs when thwarted. As pointed out by Maslow, "man lives by bread alone", when there is no bread. Physiological needs dominate when all needs are unsatisfied.

(b) Safety Needs

These are needs for a person's self-preservation and for the preservation of those dependent upon him. These needs refer to protection from physiological dangers (fire, accident), economic security (fringe benefits, health, insurance programmes) etc. Maslow stressed emotional as well as physical safety. Thus, these needs are concerned with protection from hazards of life; from danger, deprivation and threat. Safety needs are primarily satisfied through economic behaviour.

(c) Social Needs

These needs are those, which are concerned with one's relations with others. These are the needs for companionship, affection, the need to love and be loved and co- operation.

(d) Esteem Needs

These are needs for self-confidence, achievement, competence, self-respect, knowledge and for independence and freedom.

(e) Self-Actualization Needs

These are the needs for realizing one's own potentialities for continued self-development, for being creative in the broadest sense of that term. "Self fulfilling people are rare individuals who come close to living up to their full potential for being realistic, accomplishing things, enjoying life, and generally exemplifying classic human virtues".

According to Maslow's 'Need Hierarchy Concept', the behaviour of any person is dominated and determined by the most basic needs, which are unfulfilled. The higher needs are later developed and less urgent. The individuals satisfy their needs systematically, starting with most basic needs and moving up to higher order social esteem and self-actualization needs.

Maslow suggested that the various levels are inter-dependent and overlapping; each higher need emerging before the lower level need has been completely satisfied. Thus, jobs, which are able to satisfy more of the Moslow needs, would be jobs, which would result in greater satisfaction to the employee. Although there is reasonable support for Moslow's theory of Hierarchy of needs, Herzberg, Mausner and Synderman are critical of it. It is argued that Maslow's self-actualisation needs are not relevant to the large mass of humanity, especially to the working class.

(2) Frederic Herzberg's two-factor Theory:

This original study was concerned with an investigation of factors causing job satisfaction and dissatisfaction amongst engineers and accountants. Herzberg asked some engineers and accountants to think of a time, when they felt especially good about their job and a time when they felt especially bad about their jobs and to describe the conditions which led to those feelings. Herzberg (1959) [24] found that employees named different types of conditions for good and bad feelings i.e. if a feeling of achievement led to a good feeling, lack of achievement was rarely given as cause for bad feelings.

According to Herzberg, man has two different categories of needs, which are essentially independent of each other and affect behaviour in different ways. When people feel dissatisfied about their job, they are concerned about the environment in which they are working. On the other hand, when people feel good about their job, this has to do with the work itself. Herzberg calls the first category of needs as hygienic factors, because they describe man's environment and serve the primary function of preventing job dissatisfaction. He calls the second category of needs as motivators, since they seem to be effective in motivating people to superior performance.

Herzberg concluded that some job conditions operate primarily to dissatisfy employees, when these are absent, but when they are present, they do not motivate employees in a strong way. These dissatisfiers are called hygienic or maintenance factors in the job, because they are necessary to maintain a reasonable level of satisfaction in employees.

Another set of job conditions operates primarily to build strong motivation and high satisfaction, but their absence proves strongly dissatisfying. These conditions are known as motivational factors or satisfiers.

Motivational factors such as achievement and responsibility mostly are directly related to the job itself, the employees' performance and the recognition and growth that is secured from it. Motivators are mostly job centered: they are related to job content.

Figure1: HERZBERG'S TWO-FACTOR THEORY

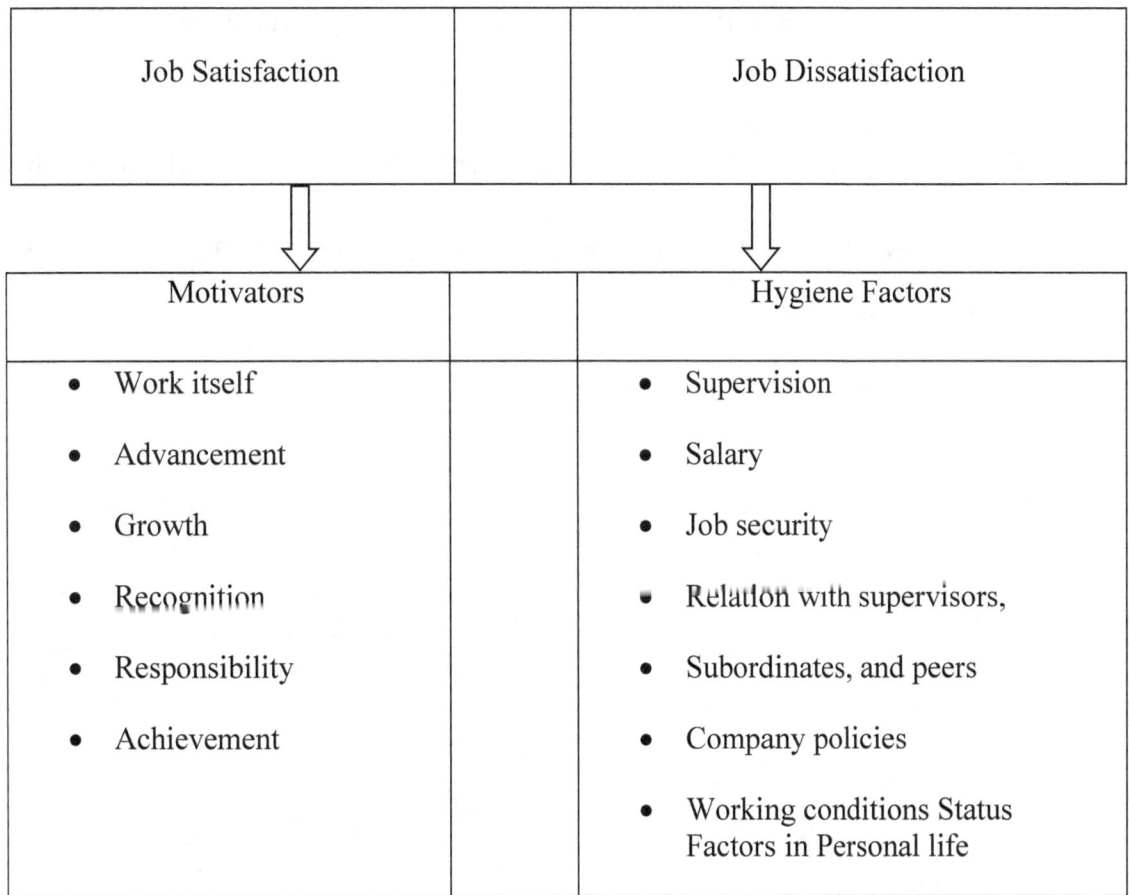

Job Satisfaction		Job Dissatisfaction

Motivators		Hygiene Factors
• Work itself • Advancement • Growth • Recognition • Responsibility • Achievement		• Supervision • Salary • Job security • Relation with supervisors, • Subordinates, and peers • Company policies • Working conditions Status Factors in Personal life

Maintenance factors related to the environment are external to the job. Thus environment includes, company policy and working conditions as well as interpersonal relations with others. Maintenance factors are environment centered: they are related to job context.

The distinction between job content and job context is similar to the distinction between intrinsic and extrinsic motivators. Intrinsic motivators are internal rewards that occur at the time of performance of the work. Extrinsic motivators are external rewards that occur after or away from work, providing no direct satisfaction at the time, the work is performed.

(3) VROOM'S EXPECTANCY THEORY

Victor Vroom (196 4) [25] proposed Valence – Instrumentality – Expectancy (VIE) Theory of satisfaction.

Valence: the strength of a person's preference for one outcome in relation to others

Expectancy: the extent to which the person believes that his efforts will lead to the first level outcome, that is, performance.

Instrumentality: refers to the degree to which a first level outcome will lead to a desired second level outcome.

Person possessing preference   Goals and associated outcomes

Among various outcomes

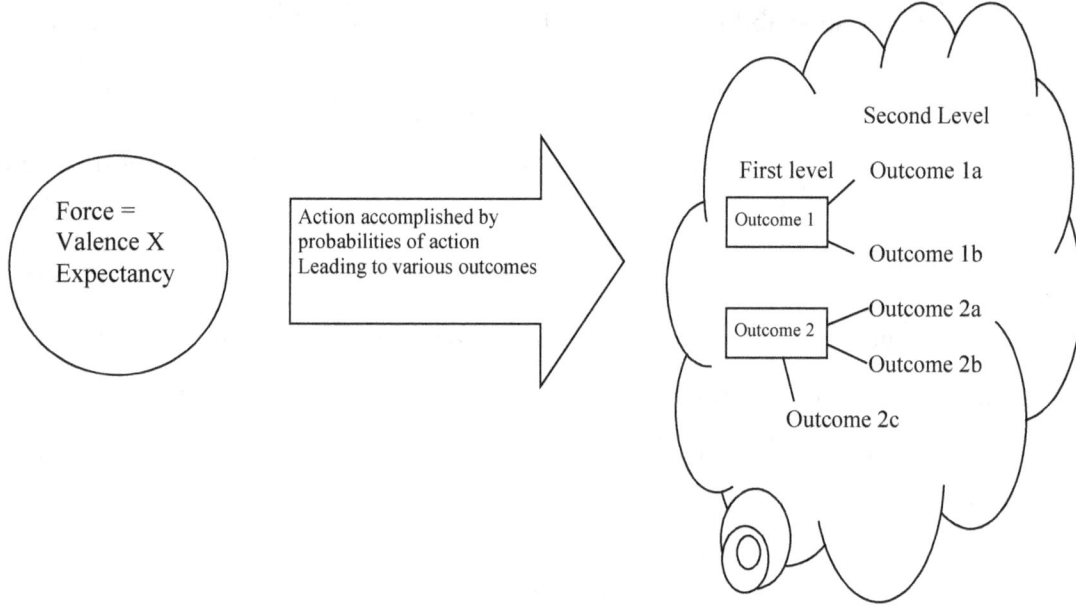

Figure 2. Vroom's Motivational Model

On the basis of the concept of expectancy, valence and instrumentality, it is possible to build the general model of behaviour as presented above. Vroom's concept of force is essentially equivalent to motivation. Expectancy and valence combine multiplicatively to determine motivation. If expectancy, valence or both equal zero, motivation will be zero. The model shows motion as the force on individuals to extend effort. However, effort will be expended only if the individual believes or feels confident that effort will lead to some performance level (performance-outcome expectancy indicated by the arrow). The level of performance is highly important in obtaining desired outcomes, which have positive valences.

4) Locke's Value Theory:

A second significant theory of job satisfaction is the value theory proposed by Locke (1984). [26] He proposed that job satisfaction occurs when the job outcomes or that which the employee receives matches with outcomes that are desired by him. The theory focuses on any outcome that people value regardless of their quality or quantity. Thus, the value attached to outcome is more important. The better the outcome that they get, the more satisfied they will be; and the less valuable outcome they receive, the less satisfied they will be. Essential to Locke's theory is, therefore, the discrepancy between the present aspect of the job and those that an employee desires such as pay, learning opportunities, promotion, and so on. Locke's value theory has been substantiated by a study of McFarlin and Rice, (1992). One of the valuable implications of the theory is that it focuses attention on those aspects of the jobs that need to be changed for employees to experience satisfaction. People perceive serious discrepancies between the job and job satisfaction. But it also suggests that these factors may not be the same for all.

(5) The Met Expectations Theory

This approach is based on the expectations that new employees have about the job and how far these expectations are met. It suggests that the employees will work to achieve the outcomes they expect to follow after successful performance (Porter and Steers, 1973). Workers become dissatisfied if their expectations about their job are not met. Review of the theory suggests that the correlation between job satisfaction and met expectations is around 0.39 (Wanous et al, 1992). One of the implications of the Met Expectations theory is that one way of reducing potential dissatisfaction among employees is to bring their expectations in line with the reality. The idea of Met Expectations suggests that the processes undergoing within the person influence job dissatisfaction. A critical viewpoint of this notion is that it ignores the social context of the individual, and this is the basis of the Equity theory.

The above five theories are discussed the following pages; motivation could be defined as an inner state that activates, energizes or moves behaviour towards goals. It is the core of management. An incentive is anything which incites or tends to incite towards some specific goals. A need is an internal state that makes certain outcomes attractive. Motive refers to the activised, need, or activised desire. The needs are of two types primary and secondary. The theritical approaches to motivation include; (1) cognitive and (2) non-cognitive. The cognitive approaches include content theories and process theories. The content theories try to answer the questions like what motivates the people. The process theories place emphasis on identification of key variables that explain individual behaviour. The process theorist concentrates on "how" motivation occurs.

According to Maslow need hierarchy model the hierarchy includes:

(1) Basic physiological needs

(2) Safety an security needs

(3) Social needs

(4) Esteem and status needs

(5) Self fulfillment needs

Herzberg and his associates put forth motivation hygiene model. The hygienic factors include wages, fringe benefits, physical conditions etc. the other factors are called motivators. According Victor Vroom Valence – Expectancy theory, there are three important features/ variables which are function of performance / motivation. The three variables are; (1) valence, (2) expectancy and (3) instrumentality. The valence is the strength of an individual's preference for a reward. Expectancy is the probability that particular action will lead to a desired reward. Instrumentality means an individual's estimate that performance will result in achieving the reward. The Porter and Lawler theory is the extension and refinement of Vroom's work and explains the important cognitive variables and how they relate to one another in the complex process of work motivation. It also gives specific attention to important relationship between performance and satisfaction; they propose that performance leads to satisfaction instead of human relation assumption of the reverse.

Locke's Value Theory: He proposed that job satisfaction occurs when the job outcomes or that which the employee receives matches with outcomes that are desired by him. The theory focuses on any outcome that people value regardless of their quality or quantity. Thus, the value attached to outcome is more important. The better the outcome that they get, the more satisfied they will be; and the less valuable outcome they receive.

The Met Expectations theory approach is based on the expectations that new employees have about the job and how far these expectations are met. It suggests that the employees will work to achieve the outcomes they expect to follow after successful performance

Determinants of Job Satisfaction

Organisations can influence job satisfaction and prevent absenteeism and turnover only if the organizations can pinpoint the factors causing and influencing these responses. Job satisfaction is derived from and is caused by many interrelated factors. Researchers – through theoretical speculation and factor analytic procedure – have identified a number of factors of job satisfaction. Some components of job satisfaction repeatedly emerged in studies whereas some varied from study to study

Hoppock (1935)[27]: Proposed six major components of job satisfaction: these include

(a) The way the individual reacts to unpleasant situations.

(b) The facility with which he adjusts himself to other persons.

 (c) His relative status in the social and economic group with which he identifies himself.

(d) The nature of work in relation to the abilities, interests and preparations.

(e) Security and

(f) Loyalty.

Scott et al. (1960)[28]: have indicated 10 important job factors to be associated with job satisfaction. These are: pay, co-workers, supervision, and type of work, working conditions, identification with the company, over-all job satisfaction, security, management and opportunity for advancement.

Siegel (1962)[29]: On the basis of his review of job satisfaction studies, he concluded that all the factors may be grouped under two headings – intrinsic and extrinsic factors. Factors intrinsic to job include pay, job security, participation and personal recognition, hours and working conditions and occupational status. Extrinsic factors are perception about supervision, sex, and age level of intelligence, job experience and personal adjustment.

Harrell (1964)[30]: Classified job satisfaction factors fall broadly into the following categories

(1) Personal factors – age, sex, number of dependents, time on the job, intelligence, education and personality.

(2) Factors inherent in the job – type of work, skills required, occupational status, geography and size of the plant, and

(3) Factors controlled by the management – security, pay, fringe benefits and opportunity for advancement, working conditions, co-workers, responsibility and supervision.

Mumford (1972)[31]: Gave a comprehensive and lengthy list of factors of job satisfaction by classifying them into three groups. Each group was identified as being composed of a number of variables. They are

(a) Organisationsl variables: the situation in which an employee works related to the organizational variable. The following are the organization variables.

(1) Size of the organization

(2) Ownership

(3) Organisational structure

(4) Inter-personal relationships

(5) Attitude towards management

24

(b) Personal Demographic and employee background variables: the individual and his background both on the job as well as outside the job. They are

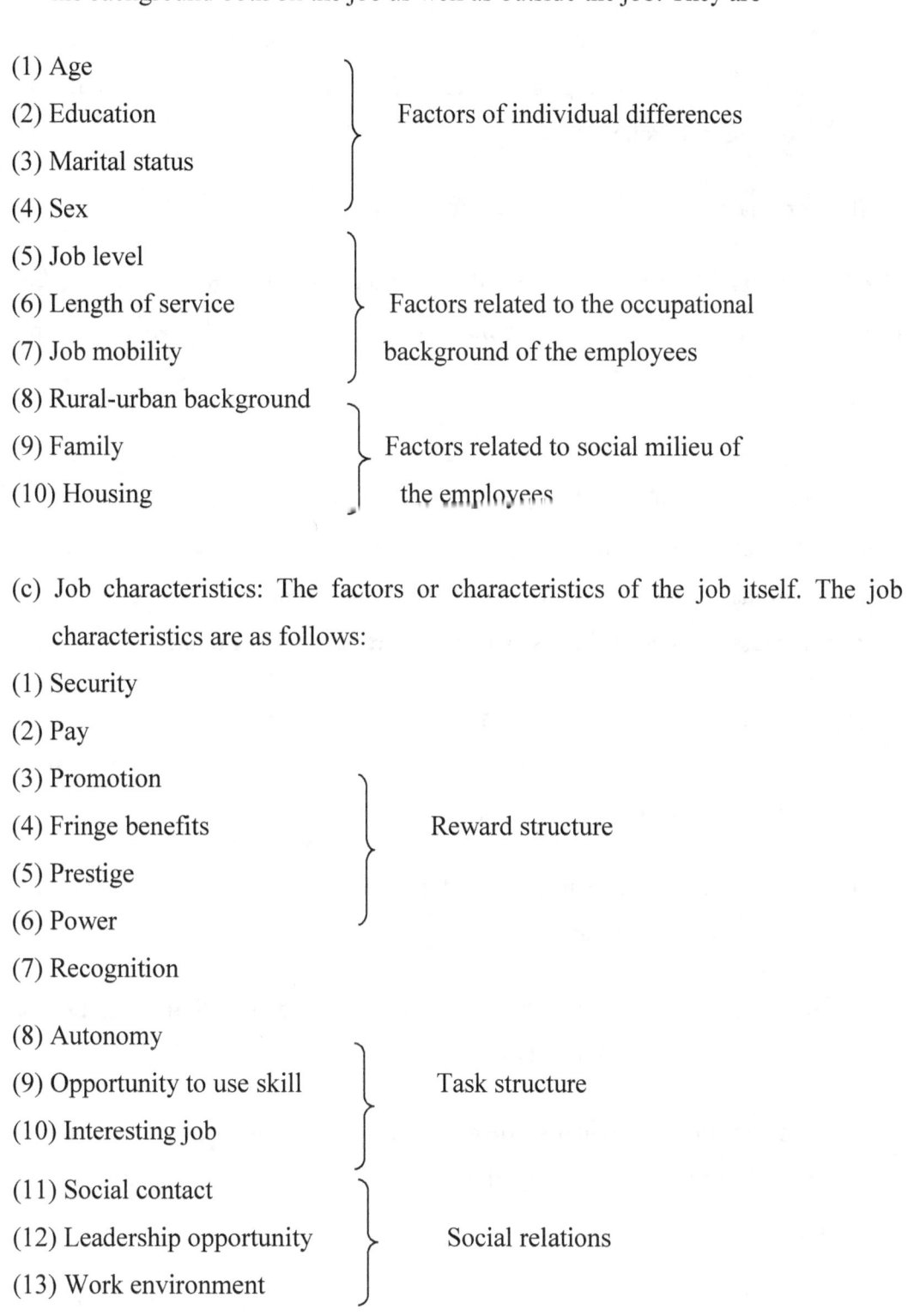

(1) Age
(2) Education
(3) Marital status
(4) Sex

⎫ Factors of individual differences

(5) Job level
(6) Length of service
(7) Job mobility

⎫ Factors related to the occupational background of the employees

(8) Rural-urban background
(9) Family
(10) Housing

⎫ Factors related to social milieu of the employees

(c) Job characteristics: The factors or characteristics of the job itself. The job characteristics are as follows:

(1) Security
(2) Pay
(3) Promotion
(4) Fringe benefits
(5) Prestige
(6) Power

⎫ Reward structure

(7) Recognition

(8) Autonomy
(9) Opportunity to use skill
(10) Interesting job

⎫ Task structure

(11) Social contact
(12) Leadership opportunity
(13) Work environment

⎫ Social relations

Korman (1978)[32]: Classified correlates of job satisfaction into two categories

(a) Environmental effects: Occupational level, job content, considerate leadership, pay and promotional opportunities, social interaction and working in a group.

(b) Personal variables: Age, sex and educational level.

Fred Luthans (1989)[33]: Enumerated six major factors that influence job satisfaction – pay, the work itself, promotions, supervision, and the workgroup and working conditions.

Pestonjee (1991)[34]: In a review of job satisfaction studies, identified that both on-the-job factors and off-the-job factors consist of two subsets, which are again composed of many intertwined job aspects. For e.g. job and management areas comprise on-the-job factors. Likewise, personal adjustment and social relations areas encompass off-the-job factors. These four areas with their related aspects are:

(a) Job area: Nature of work, hours of work, fellow workers, opportunities on the job for promotion and advancement, over-time regulations, interest in work, physical environment, machines and tools etc.

(b) Management area: Supervisory treatment, participation, rewards and punishment, praises and blames, leave policy, favoritism.

(c) Personal adjustment: Emotionality, health, home and living conditions, finances, relation with family members etc.

(d) Social relations: Neighbors, friends and associates, attitudes towards people in the community, participation in social activities, sociability, caste barriers etc.

From the foregoing discussion, it is evident that job satisfaction is a complex phenomenon affected by many inter-related variables. Research studies have identified a number of factors. Some of these factors of job satisfaction have repeatedly emerged in these studies whereas some varied from study to study. Also it is observed that the importance of various factors appears to change from one situation to another. There are many factors, but only those considered most important are discussed here.

FACTORS OF JOB SATISFACTION FOR THE PRESENT STUDY

Keeping in view the factors enumerated in different studies, for the purpose of present research study the factors affecting job satisfaction can be broadly classified under two heads.

(1) Personal factors

(2) Job related factors

These factors are briefly discussed in the following pages.

(1) PERSONAL FACTORS

(A) Age

The relationship between age of the employees and their satisfaction from the Job is both complex and fascinating. Research reveals that old workers are satisfied workers. Job satisfaction usually tends to be high when people enter the work force; it plummetes and the plateaus for several years, (say for five to six years) up to the age of roughly thirty years, after which there will be gradual increase in satisfaction. Another plausible reason could be people, when they begin their job-life, have a tendency of over estimating themselves and seek flexibility and what to be placed in good organizations. After some period, when they get settled down in a particular job, they become realistic and may be content with it. But certainly just before retirement, satisfaction may fall due to the fear of future.

(b) Sex

The results of several studies relating to job satisfaction seem to indicate that women are more satisfied with their job than men. This is so despite the fact that women are generally discriminated against in job competition and pay. The reason for it might be those women's ambitions and financial needs are less. But some other studies indicated that men are more satisfied than women.

(c) Education Level

Keeping the occupational level as constant, they found a negative correlation between the level of education of employees and their satisfaction. One plausible explanation could be that people with higher educational levels have higher expectations from their jobs. Dissatisfaction will be more when educated persons are employed in lower rungs.

(d) Job Level / Designation

The higher the level of the job, the greater the job satisfaction. People in higher-level occupations are better paid and have better working conditions, and their jobs make fuller use of their abilities; therefore, they have good reasons to be more satisfied.

(d) Marital Status

Some studies reported that married employees expressed more job satisfaction than did the unmarried ones. This may be because married adults have better adjustment than unmarried counterparts.

(e) Family Size

According to some studies, size of the family also is found to have an effect on job satisfaction. Employees with less number of dependents were found to be more satisfied with their job.

(f) Experience

Several investigations have revealed that there is a positive relationship between experience and job satisfaction. Employees with greater experience tend to be more satisfied with their jobs. This is because their better adjustment to the work situation stems from experience with it. The length of service in the organization broadens the knowledge of the employees about the organization and develops a sort of loyalty and attachment to the concern.

(g) Geographical Background

Employees having urban background are less satisfied with their jobs when compared to the employees having rural background. This is due to the reason that employees with urban background have more expectations from the job, which would result in lower satisfaction. On the other hand, the expectations of the employees with rural background are less and, as a result, their job satisfaction would be high.

JOB RELATED FACTORS

1. Nature of Work

Most employees crave intellectual challenges on their jobs. Therefore, they prefer jobs that offer them challenges and an opportunity to use their skill and abilities. However, while too much challenge in job creates frustration and feelings of failure, too little challenge causes boredom. In fact, it is the conditions of moderate challenge in which employees experience pleasure and satisfaction.

2. Salary and Promotion

Employees want their salary system and promotion policies as unambiguous and in line with their expectations. Accordingly, if they see pay, as fair, based on job demands and employees skill and as per community pay standards, it results in job satisfaction.

Not surprisingly, employees consider promotions as their ultimate achievement in their craves. When they achieve it, they feel satisfied with their jobs. Besides, promotions made on a fair and just manner are also likely to create job satisfaction for the employees.

3. Supervision

Cordial and Supportive personal relationships with subordinates lead one to take interest in subordinates' well-being. These characteristics of supervision create satisfaction for employees in their jobs.

4. Supportive Colleagues

Experience shows that employees get more out of work than only money or tangible achievements. It happens primarily by having opportunities for interaction with colleagues. Work team fills the need for social interaction. Thus, having supportive colleagues also leads to employee's job satisfaction.

5. Working Conditions

Employees are concerned with their environment for both personal, comfort and facilitating doing a job. Therefore, the physical surroundings that are safe, clean, comfortable and with a minimum degree of distribution result in good or positive feelings.

6. Recognition

Recognition for work is another significant factor of job satisfaction. Most of the people have need for a high evaluation of themselves. They feel that others concerned should recognize what they do. Recognition means acknowledgment with a show of appreciation. When the work performed by the employees is appreciated, they feel elated and satisfied.

7. Status and Prestige

Prestige and status derived form the job affects the level of satisfaction of an employee with his hob. The status depends not only on the way the employee regards the status of his job, but also on the way others whose opinion he values regard it. Normally people prefer jobs with higher status in the society

8. Opportunity for Advancement

Opportunity to develop one has some modest effect on satisfaction of an employee. This factor includes all those job aspects, which the individual sees as potential sources of betterment of economic position, organizational status, or professional experience.

9. Sense of Achievements

Generally people have an inner urge to achieve something. The sense of achievements depends upon opportunity to achieve, level of motivation and environment prevailing in the organization. When the employees attain something remarkable, they feel extremely happy and satisfied. As such, sense of achievement in the job is one of the factors that moderately affects the level of satisfaction of employees.

10. Welfare Facilities

Welfare facilities should be provided to the employees for their maintenance in happiness, health and prosperity. These include medical, educational, housing, transport, marketing facilities etc. They influence job satisfaction of the employees.

11. Responsibility

Responsibility is usually enmeshed with several other important determinants of job satisfaction in a way that makes it difficult to determine the relative contribution of each to job satisfaction. Responsibility usually goes with time on the job, age, salary, type of work and participation, and it may have some relation to interest. One study of employees all over the U.S. showed that moral scores were higher for employees who had more responsibility. So this unit must be strengthened.

REFERENCES

1. G. James Francis and Gene Milbourn, Jr., **Human Behaviour in the Work Environment: A Managerial Perspective,** Goodyear Publishing Co., Santa Monica, California, 1980, p 92.

2. Joe Kelly, **Organizational Behaviour**, Richard D. Irwin, Inc, Illinois, 1980, p.483.

3. Benjamin Schneider and Rover A. Snyder, "Some Relations Between Job Satisfaction and Organizational Climate, **Journal of Applied Psychology**, 60, No.3. 1975. P.318.

4. G.A. Forehand and B. Von H. Gilmer "Environmental Variations in Studies of Organisational Behaviour." **Psychological Bulletin,** Vol.62, No.6, December 1964, pp.361-382.

5. Litwin, G.H. and Stringer, R.A.: **Motivation and Organisational Climate**. Boston, Division of Research, Graduate School of Business Administration, Harvard University, 1968, pp.213-215.

6. Campbell, J.P, Dunnette, M.D, Lawler, E.E, and Weick K.E. Jr "**Managerial Behaviour, Performance and Effectiveness**", New York: Mc Graw Hill, 1970, p.390.

7. Baumgartel. H. 'The Perception of Modern Management Technology and Organisational Practices in Indian Business Organisation", **Indian Administrative and Management Review**, No.3, 1971, p.2.

8. G.A. Forehand and B. Von H. Gilmer, op.cit, p.361 -382.

9. G.H. Litwin and R. Stringer. "The Influence of Organisational Climate on Human Motivation". Paper presented in Organisational Climate, Foundation for Research on **Human Behaviour**, March 1966, Quoted in Climate et al. op. cit, p.391.

10. Likert, R.: **The Human Organization**. New York: McGraw Hill, 1967, p.113.

11. B. Schneider and C.J. Bartlett, "Individual differences and Organisaational Climate." **Personnel Psychology**, No. 21, 1968, pp. 323-334.

12. R. Taguiri, "**Comments on Organisational Climate**," Quoted in Campbell et al. op.cit. p. 392.

13. Pritchard Robert D., and Bernard W. Karasick. "The Effects of Orgnisational Climate on Managerial Job performance and Job Satisfaction," **Organisational Behaviour and Human Performance,** Vol.9. 1973. pp. 126-146.

14. Lawrence R. James and Allan P. Jones, "Organisational Climate, A Review of Theory and Research," **Psychological Bulletin**, Vol. 81, Dec., 1974, p. 1098.

15. John E.Newman, "Development of a Measure of Perceived Work Environment", **Academy of Management Journal**, Vol.20, No.4, 1977, pp.520-534.

16. U. Pareek, **Motivational Analysis of Organization's** Climate in Developing Human Resources, Annual, 1987, University Association, San Diego, pp. 160-180.

17. Hodgetts, Richhard M. **"Organisational Behviour**: Theory and Practice", Macmillan Publishing, 1991, PP.428-430.

18. Hoppock. R., **"Job Satisfaction"**, Harper and Row, New York, 1935. p.42

19. Bullock, R.P., "Social factors related to job satisfaction", Research Monograph, No. 70, **Bureau of Business Research**, Ohio State University, Columbus, 1952, p.92.

20. Smith H.C., **"Psychology of Industrial Behaviour"**, McGraw Hill, New York, 1955. p.46

21. Davis, K., **"Human Behaviour** at Work: Organisational Behaviour", (Sixth Edition), Tata McGraw Hill Publishing Company Ltd., 1977, p.145.

22. Pestonjee, D.M., "**Motivation and Job Satisfaction**", McMillan India Ltd., New Delhi, 1991.

23. Maslow, A.H., A Theory of Human Motivation", **Psychological Review**", Vol.50, 1943, pp. 370-396.

24. Herzberg, F., Mausner, B., and Synderman, B.B., "**The Motivation to Work**", New York, John Wiley, 1959.

25. Vroom, V.H., **Work and Motivation**, New York, John Wiley and Sons, 1964.

26. Locke, **Job satisfaction**. In M. Gruenberg and Y. Wall (eds) Social Psychology and Organizational Behaviour; (London: Wiley), 1984, pp.22-28

27. Hoppock. R., op.cit., p.42.

28. Scott, T.B., Davis, R.V., England, G.W. and Lofquist, L.H., A Definition of Work Adjustment, Minnesota Studies in Vocational Rehabilitation: **Industrial Relations Centre**, University of Minnesota, Minnesota, 1960.

29. Siegel, L., **Industrial Psychology**, Irwin, Homewood, 1962.

30. Harrell, T.W., **Industrial Psychology**, Oxford Book Company, Calcutta, 1964.

31. Mumford, E., **job Satisfaction** – A Study of Computer Specialists, Longman, 1972, p.82.

32. Korman, A.K., **Organisational Behaviour**, Prentice Hall of India, Private Ltd., New Delhi, 1978, pp.18-21.

33. Luthans, F., **Organizational Behaviour** (Fifth Edition), McGraw Hill Series in Management, 1 989, pp.82-89.

34. Pestonjee, D.M., op.cit., p.42

Chapter - II

REVIEW OF LITERATURE AND METHODOLOGY

In this chapter an attempt is made to review some of the earlier studies on organizational climate and job satisfaction and outline the review of literature, statement of the problem need of the study, significance of the study, objectives of the study, hypotheses formulated, scope of the study, selection of sample, method of data collection, statistical tools used for data analysis, and limitations of the study.

Studies on job satisfaction can perhaps be said to have begun in earnest with the publication of Elton Mayo's pioneering work, popularly known as "Hawthorne Studies" in 1930s[1]. These studies can be considered as the pace setters for increasing interest in the study of human relations. The complete Hawthorne studies were done in a series of experiments viz., illumination Experiments, Relay Room Experiments and Bank Writing Room Experiments conducted between 1927 and 1932. Although these experiments may not be regarded as 'acme of performance', yet they are honest and concerted efforts to understand employees, instead of approaching the problem only from managerial point of view of increasing efficiency on an economic level. These experiments established the significance of the human relationship within the work organization.

Frederiksen[2] on the basis of laboratory studies involving 260 middle-level managers, concluded that different types of organizational climate have different effects on human performance. He summarized his findings with the following statements. It appears that the amount of administrative work in the simulated job is more predictable in a climate that encourages innovation than in one that encourages standard procedures, and that, in an innovative climate (but not in a rules climate) greater productivity can be expected of people with skills and attitudes that are associated with independence of thought and action.

REVIEW OF LITERATURE

A review of the research studies on organizational climate and job satisfaction abroad has been classified into three sections i.e., dependent variable, independent variable and intervening variable.

A brief review of literature of the three categories of studies is attempted here, though the present study is related to the first category of research works.

Dependent Variable

Studies on Education Sector

Natarajan (2001)[3]: In his article "A study on Organizational Climate and Teacher Morale", finds out the relationship between the school organizational climate and the morale of teachers. Climates are found to be equal in numbers the familiar climate among is found to be the least in number. Teacher morale is found to be the highest in open climate among all types of school climate. It is interesting to note that the teacher morale of the outcomes and controlled climate is the same, but the teacher moral declines continuously from open to closed climate.

Sumanlata (2005)[4]: In her article "A Study of Educational Attainment as a Function of School Organizational Climate", made an attempt results indicates that significant difference between educational attainment of different types of organizational climate. School climate influences the educational attainment and develop abilities in the pupils. The organizational climate of a school has three important variables – principal, teacher and pupil's joint contribution of these variables constitutes the organizational climate of the school. Thus the climate of a school differs from one to another has a direct effect upon the educational attainment of the pupils.

Sharma and Jeevan Jyoti (2006)[5]: In their article "Job Satisfaction Among School Teachers", tried an analysis of the dimensions of job satisfaction. Their study indicates that job security and a guiding approach by the principal towards his subordinates add to the job satisfaction of government secondary school teachers. On the other hand, underestimation of the profession by society and the antisocial elements among the students lead to dissatisfaction.

Private primary school teachers have secured the maximum satisfaction from the students and the physical environment and minimum satisfaction from the pay and rewards dimension. The reason for their dissatisfaction is probably their high qualification but low job status. They further reported that their position does not match their experiences.

(I) Studies on Banks and Hospitals

Lyon and Ivancevich (1974)[6]: In their article "An Exploratory Investigation of Organizational Climate and Job Satisfaction in a Hospital". The empirical study finds that organizational climate for both occupational groups has the most significant impact on (self actualization personal growth sense of accomplishment advancement opportunity and challenging work), a lesser impact on autonomy (setting goals and using training and experience) and a slight impact on esteem (importance with in and outside of the hospital)

Akhilesh and Pandey (1986)[7]: In their article, "A Comparative Study of Organizational Climate in Two Banks", conducted a comparative study. This indicates that Nationalized Bank has a better attitudinal profile over private sector Bank. Private sector bank perceived the strongest relationship between "recognition and positive record and performance" when compared to the perceptions of executives from the nationalized bank. In other words there is better recognition and reward for performance in the private sector bank. It could be said that the private sector bank has a slightly task oriented climate.

Jahan and Haque (1993)[8]: Made a critical study on "Effects of Organizational Climate on Job Related Aspects of Middle Level Managers of Banks". The authors observed and found that there is an indispensable correlation between job satisfaction and the organizational factors like decision making, communication, supervision and salary packages.

Gani and Shah (2001)[9]: Conducted a study on the Banking Industry in the State of Jammu and Kashmir. The total employees in all the banks in aggregate were about 3745. The total size of the sample was restricted to 125. The stratified sampling technique was employed for drawing the sample. The authors provided an adequate description of the concept, constructed determinants and correlates of organisational climate. The study indicated that the banking industry as a whole has a poorly perceived organizational climate and that the situation in the private sector banks is worse than that in public sector ones.

(II) Studies in manufacturing sector

Sinha and Sharma (1962)[10]: In their article, "Union Attitude and Job Satisfaction in Indian Workers", found that no relationship between attitude towards union and job satisfaction of the personal factors – age, marital status, and length of union membership were significantly related to job satisfaction.

A study conducted by Guha (1965)[11]: in his article, "Job Satisfaction among Shoe Factory Workers", observed the relationship between job satisfaction and introversion – extroversion. The study found that extroversion leads to more satisfaction, married workers are more satisfied than the unmarried workers and that there is significant negative relationship between job satisfaction and neuroticism.

Nataraj and Hafeez (1965)[12]: In their article "A Study of Job Satisfaction Among Skilled Workers", made an attempt to study the skilled workers found besides are satisfied with their jobs and to study how for the factors of age, salary, experience, education etc., influenced job satisfaction.

Peterson (1975)[13]: In his article, "The Interaction of Technological Process and Perceived Organizational Climate in Norwegian Firms", made an attempt to study the more open climate in small batch and process technologies than for mass assemblies.

Study conducted by Pallavi Shah (1976)[14] in her article, "Need Importance and Need Fulfillment in Management Levels", concluded that

1. All three management levels accord high importance to esteem, autonomy and self actualization needs.

2. The autonomy and self-actualization needs are not adequately fulfilled in any one of the three levels, and

3. Self-actualization is the most important need at all the managerial levels and this need is least adequately met.

Klaleque and Choudhury (1984)[15] in their article "Job Facets and Overall Job Satisfaction of Industrial Managers", found in their study that the top managers had considered the nature of the work as the most important factor fringe benefit is the least important factor for job satisfaction. On the other hand, the bottom managers had considered job security as the most important factor and wage as the least important factor in job satisfaction. It was found that the mean scores of overall job satisfaction are high for both the top and bottom managers in terms of their satisfaction.

Sharma and Venkata Ratnam (1987)[16] in their article, "Organizational Climate and Supervisory-Management Relations in Bharat Ispat Nigam", observed major between the outcomes of the two modes of analysis of the nine dimensions of climate studied (Safety & Security, Monetary Benefits, Objectivity & Rationality, Recognition and Appreciation, Warfare Facilities, Scope for Advancement, Grievance Handling, Training & Education, and Participative Management) only two grievance handling and objectivity emerged as the critical determinants of Supervisory-Management relations.

Sebastian and Bhargava (2003)[17] in their article " Organizational Climate of Non- Profit Organization", result show that using individual perception to measure organizational climate was considered adequate in his study, field staff gave higher rating than office staff because their involvement in the non-profit organization was higher, field staff are mostly females but the administrative and authoritative positions are held by males, close supervision was not a threat in non-profit organization; it was the absence of supervision and guidance that was plaguing the employees.

In an empirical study conducted by Avinash Kumar (2006)[18] in his article "Organizational Climate in Public Sector: An Empirical Study", organizational climate comprising three functional motives (achievement expert influence and extension) and three dysfunctional motives (dependency, control and affiliation) was measured for 453 randomly selected respondents from a large public sector industry, using MAO- C instrument. Dependency has been found to be the dominant climate. Affiliation is the back up climate, extension climate is the weakest in the organization. Strong interrelations exist among the six climate motives, except for the pairs; expert influence-extension, extension-affiliation and control-affiliation which are not correlated. With the exception of dependency-affiliation pair, these correlations are

40

found to be positive. When both the variables in the pair represent functional climate or when both of them represent dysfunctional climate. On the other hand, they are negative when one of the variables involved represents functional climate and the other variable represents dysfunctional climate. Dependency is negatively correlated with affiliation even though both these represent dysfunctional climate.

A cross functional study was conducted by Avinash Kumar Srivastav (2007)[19] He in his article, "Achievement Climate in Public Sector – A Cross Functional Study on Relationship with Stress and Coping", shows that people with a high need for achievement prefer to work in the private sector and those with low need for achievement prefer to work in the public sector. Several factors make achievement of organizational goals more difficult in the pubic sector. Individual and organizational resistance to change is stronger in the public sector and individuals with strong achievement needs react positively when they are responsible for the accomplishment of challenging but achievable goals and when their innovative and entrepreneurial behaviors are rewarded. Thus individual need for achievement and organizational climate are significant determinants of individual performance in organizations,

Bahadur katuwal and Gurprect Randhawa (2007)[20] in their article, " Study of Job Satisfaction of Public and Private Sector Nepalese Textile Workers", found the public sector textile workers to be statistically most satisfied than their counterparts in private sector in terms of personal policies, participatory management, behavior of friends, and welfare facilities. The private sector textile workers were found more satisfied than the public sector textile workers in terms of duration of work, wage, job security and training development.

Independent Variable and Dependent Variable

The influences of organizational climate on job satisfaction, motivation and performance are highlighted here.

(a) Studies on Organizational Climate and Job Satisfaction

Chatterji (1960)[21] pointed out that modern society recognizes the importance of every individual experiencing satisfaction in his/her job. Job security, a good supervision, opportunities, for promotion and satisfactory solutions of grievances are as important as amount of pay.

Singh and Singh (1961)[22]: Conducted a study on 90 supervisors. The results indicated that personal factors like age, marital status, education and number of dependents have significant effect on the level of job satisfaction.

Ewen (1964)[23]: In his article, "Some Determinants of Job Satisfaction: A Study of the Generality of Herzberg's Theory", analysed the impact of the certain work situation variables i.e., recognition, achievement interesting work, responsibility and advancement all lead to positive job attitudes while other variables i.e. company policy and administration, supervision, and working conditions will not lead to positive job attitudes.

Frank Friedlander (1964)[24]: In his article ,"Job Characteristics as Satisfiers and Dissatisfiers", made an attempt to examine the job characteristics such as achievement, challenging, recognition, and the work itself were viewed as most important to both satisfaction and dissatisfaction. Work characteristics least important to both satisfaction and dissatisfaction were employee benefits, merit increases, working conditions, effect of job on home life, job security and the technical competence of the supervisor.

Sarveswara Rao and Ganapathi Rao (1973)[25]: In their article "A Study of Factors Contributing to Satisfaction and Importance of Industrial Personnel: A Test of the Two Factor Theory", made an empirical investigation of two factory theory of job satisfaction. Using multivariable analysis they revealed that motivators and hygiene were not mutually exclusive variables and their effects were not unidirectional. Both motivators and hygiene contributed to overall satisfaction and both the variables were considered important in their relationship to the dependent variable.

Sushila Singhal (1973)[26]: In his article " Measurement of Job Satisfaction on a Three – Dimensional Plane", carried out an empirical investigation on the three types of factors that interacted with and influenced each other, and did exercise a significant influence on job satisfaction index a combination of measures into indices of personal, work, and social adjustment, than between personal and work adjustment, through all three interrelated significantly. The principal component analysis demonstrated that the highest contribution to job satisfaction was made by work

42

adjustment and least by personal adjustment, though all the three indices remained significant in the study of job satisfaction.

Hellriegel and Slocum (1974)[27] in their article,"Organizational Climate: Measures, Research and Contingencies", made an attempt to analyse the existing literature. The possibility of interaction between other organizational variables, such as rewards, communication linkages, locus of decision making, and climate, has not been explored.

Carrell, and Elbert (1974)[28], in their article, "Some Personal and Organisational Determinants of Job Satisfaction of Postal Clerks", undertook a research on inverse relationship between educational level and satisfaction and found that those with less than a high school diploma were the most satisfied. Organizational climate should be evaluated in terms of the accuracy of the perceptions.

Schneider, (1975)[29] in his article, "Organisational Climate: An Essay", has attempted to study some logical and conceptual distinctions between job satisfaction and organizational climate.

1. It was noted that the word satisfaction implies an effective internal state while the word climate refers to a moral description of a situation.

2. The point was made that these moral descriptions are composites of practices and procedures people encounter in their work worlds; that climate is an abstraction of or a labelling of a specific set of practices and procedures.

Schneider and Snyder (1975)[30]: In their article "Some Relationship between Job Satisfaction and Organisational Climate", examined the relationships among two measures of job satisfaction, one measure of organizational climate, and seven production and turnover indexes of organizational effectiveness. These were investigated in 50 life insurance agencies (N= 522). It was shown that;

1. Climate and satisfaction measures are correlated for people in some position in the agencies but not for others;

2. People agree more on the climate of their agency than they do on their satisfaction:

3. Neither satisfaction nor climates strongly correlate with production data: and

4. Satisfaction, but not climate, is correlated with turnover data.

Payne, Fineman, and Wall (1976)[31], in their article "Organizational Climate and Job Satisfaction: A Conceptual Synthesis", predict job satisfaction will be moderately related to role morale and role climate, and perceived job characteristics are likely to be moderately related to role morale but of lower relation to role climate, another relationship will be higher is that between satisfaction with organization and perceived organizational characteristics.

Muchinsky's (1977)[32] article, "Organisational Communication: Relationship to Organizational Climate and Job Satisfaction", an exploratory study, tries to examine certain dimensions of organizational communication and finds that they were highly related to both organizational climate and job satisfaction.

Pramod Kumar and Chandrakala Bora (1979)[33] in their article "Job Satisfaction and Perceived Organizational Climate ", emphasise the perceived organizational climate tended to significantly affect job satisfaction of the workers. The workers who perceived the existing organizational climate as democratic were found to have higher satisfaction over all and area wise than workers perceiving the same climate as autocratic or undecided.

Dwivedi (1979)[34] wrote an article "Anatomy of Organizational Climate". The results have been classified into three groups.

1. The Organizational Climate has been studied as an Independent variable influencing employee satisfaction and performance

2. Organizational Climate is analysed as an Intervening variable, for example, between leadership style and employee performance or satisfaction, and

3. The Organizational Climate has been treated as a dependent variable being influenced by leadership style, technology, organizational structure, and management assumptions and practices.

Poonam Baja (1982)[35] in his article, "Alienation as Related to Perception of Organizational Climate", shows that alienation scores will have a high correlation with the perception of autocratic organizational climate, and low correlation with perception of democratic organizational climate.

Arya (1984)[36] in his article, "Work Satisfaction and its Correlation", studied worker's satisfaction in terms of seven facets of his job, namely, the satisfaction from supervisory behaviour, welfare facilities, working of the bipartite committees, wages, promotion policy, job content and identification with the company. The study revealed that education, training, workers' participation in the bipartite committees also had a positive influence over work satisfaction whereas militancy and work satisfaction had a negative relationship in both the places.

Surya Kumar Srivastava (1990)[37]: He conducted a study on "Relationship Between Job Satisfaction and Organizational Climate". The results can be stated as follows

1. Job Satisfaction is related to pay, education and nature of work. But age , and experience is not related to job satisfaction in private sector employees

2. Job Satisfaction is related to age, pay, education, and nature of work. But experience is not related to job satisfaction in public sector employees.

3. Perception of organizational climate is related to age, pay experience, education and nature of work in both sectors.

4. The relationship between job satisfaction and organization climate was found quite significant for both private and public sectors.

5. Private sector employees are better than public sector employees in terms of job satisfaction

6. The organizational climate of private sector employees was perceived to be favourable and that of public sector employees was perceived to be unfourable.

The overall picture that emerges is that things are much better in private sector as compared to public sector.

A study conducted by Dolke (1991)[38] in his article "Personal – Personality, Job and Organisational Correlates of Work Identification", result indicate that significantly related to personal variables of age and tenure, personality variables of levels of control and satisfaction of higher order needs, is also related to job related variables of challenge and autonomy. The organizational variables related to participation in departmental decision making, supervisory support, and perceived chances of rising of in the organizational hierarchy and fulfillment of higher order needs.

Sayeed (1992)[39]: In his article,"Organisational effectiveness: Relationship with Job Satisfaction Facets", revealed that job satisfaction facets had more explanatory power than the personal attributes of respondents such as age, education, pay and length of service. It was clear from the study that the organization through its human resource development policies and practices creates better environment for employees, resulting in greater satisfaction which, in turn, enhances organizational effectiveness.

Rama Davi (1997)[40]: Conducted a study on "Faculty Job Satisfaction and their Views on Management of two Universities in Andhra Pradesh". The sample consists of 200 teaching faculty -100 teaching staff working in Sri Krishnadevaraya University, Anantapur, and teaching staff working in the University of Hyderabad. The sample was drawn on random basis using Fisher and Yates random numbers and an attempt was made to measure job satisfaction of the faculty in the universities in Andhra Pradesh. It was found that factors such as freedom in doing job, scope for self improvement, income and job security cause satisfaction while bureaucratic rules, no recognition for work and routine work are the causes of dissatisfaction to them.

Taylor (2000)[41]: Suggested that job satisfaction is directly related to company's investment in employee's well being. When an organization cares for its employees, it definitely gets their support in reward. Organizational investment in employee's well being results in the higher satisfaction of employees.

Chakrapani (2001)[42]: Conducted a study on "Job Satisfaction Among Employees of Select Manufacturing Units in Cuddapah, Andhra Pradesh". The study revealed that an organization, through its human resource policies and development practices, can create better organizational environment for employees resulting in greater satisfaction which in turn leads to enhanced organizational effectiveness and efficiency. It appears that Electrolux India Ltd, unit has better organizational climate and human resource policies and practices resulting in higher job satisfaction levels among employees when compared to those in the other two units i.e., Cuddapah Spinning Mills Ltd., and Zuari Cement Ltd. under study

Sinha, and Gupta, et.al, (2001)[43]: In their article "Societal Beliefs, Organizational Climate, and Managers' Self-perceptions", examine how traditional societal beliefs affect organizational climate, and how the two, independently or jointly, shape managers' self – perceptions. It also investigates the impact of the levels of development on societal beliefs and how they affect organizational climate; but it is the organizational climate that has a deeper impact on managers' self-perceptions. The article highlights the importance of creating a work-centric and caring organization.

Sharma, et al., (2001)[44]: Carried out a study in a large Engineering Industrial Organisation and tried to find out the extent of job satisfaction of its women artisans. The study also intended to know whether the determinants of job satisfaction evoke any reaction or response from the women workers. It is found from the study that about 80 per cent of the respondents agreed that they got adequate supervisory guidance, 40 per cent of the respondents were fully satisfied with the job while 48 per cent expressed their partial satisfaction. This partial satisfaction, according to the authors, may be due to disinterest, monotony, and partiality of the supervisor and the pressure of the family. The authors concluded that job satisfaction cannot be the result of external factors but a conse intrinsic factors of the job.

Antony Joseph (2001)[45]: In his article "Job Satisfaction Among Transport Employees", assessed and found that the public sector employees are highly satisfied with salary and other allowances, job security social status, working hours and relation with passengers. The private sector employees are highly satisfied with management policies, relation with co-workers, working conditions and trade union relations.

Malik and Goyal (2003)[46]: In their article "Organizational Environment and Information System", suggested an A C E Model – a three ring model comprising process to Adapt, Collaborate and Evaluate, in order to establish and evaluate organizational effectiveness for improved information system in the organization . At the core is the need to cultivate a culture to adapt the latest tools and techniques for higher end use. Next, the people must collaborate and work in terms for faster and beneficial plans and their implementation. Finally a well-defined process for constant monitoring and refinement of the plans is required.

Bose and Agarwal (2005)[47]: wrote an article on "Organizational Work Climate and Perceived 'Procedural Fairness' of Human Resource Practices". The results of their work revealed that an organizational climate that ensures system-support for innovation, interpersonal trust between the superior and the subordinate and participation in decision making and member welfare is positively related with perception of procedural fairness among organizational members. Findings indicated that organizations, which would like to ensure members' loyalty in the context of a changing environment, should focus primarily on creating a positive work climate that can facilitate perceptions of procedural 'fairness' in their human resource practice.

Sailaja Rani (2006)[48]: Conducted a study on "Job Satisfaction Among Bank Employees in Chittoor District of A.P." The results indicate the relationship between job satisfaction and various socio-economic factors like status/cadre, age, and experience of the employees working in the banks. It is found that by and large, these factors did not affect much the level of job satisfaction, barring a few exceptions. The exceptions are; in State Bank of India, the status/ cadre of the employees had shown some impact on the level of job satisfaction, and, similarly, in Indian Overseas Bank, the length of experience of the employees also affected the job satisfaction level of its employees.

Srimannarayana (2007)[49]: in his study attempts to assess "Human Resource Development Climate in Dubai Organizations" based on the responses of 216 executives working in shipping, banking, insurance, tourism, trading and food business organization located in Dubai. He concludes that the climate is at an average level. In comparison, it is observed that the HRD climate in banking business is at a higher level than their other business. This is followed by the insurance and shipping business. Low level HRD climate is observed in tourism, food and trading organization when compared to banking, insurance and shipping organization.

A.P. Singh and Sadhana Singh (2009)[50]: Have conducted a study on 210 "Managerial personnel working in different private sector Organizations" with a view to examine the role of stress and work culture on job satisfaction. The statistics employed are Mean, Standard Deviation, t-test and bi-variate correlation. The results of bivariate correlation indicate that job positive stress and total positive stress are positively correlated with satisfaction with management and overall satisfaction(job and management), whereas personal positive stress is significantly positively correlated with overall satisfaction.

Results of t-test indicate that there is significant mean difference in satisfaction with job, satisfaction with management and overall satisfaction between high and low job positive stress, personal positive stress and total positive stress. The difference is found to be significant for satisfaction with management in the case of high and low work culture, namely, obligations towards others.

(b) Organizational Climate and Motivation

According to Sharma (1983)[51]: In his article "Employee Motivation and Employer –Employee Relations in India", he observes that grievance handling, recognition and appreciation, participative management and scope for advancement are important factors in an organizational climate enhancing work motivation of employees. In other words, what is required is an improvement in the quality of work life in industry and not merely the quantum of material benefits about which the employees already feel quite satisfied.

Archana Tarabadkar and Rehana Ghadially (1985)[52]: In their article "Achievement Motivation and Job Satisfaction", focused attention on professional men and women and non-professional men. They selected more motivators than hygienes for both satisfying and dissatisfying job situation thus partially confirming Hertzberg's two factor theory.

Srivastava (1985)[53]: In his article, " Motivation and Perception of Organizational Climate", attempts to examine the employees highly motivated by the n- Achievement, in comparison to low motivated ones. The former perceived most of the components of their job life to be comparatively more adequate, desirable and encouraging.

(c) Studies on Performance

Pritchard and karasick (1973)[54]: In their article "The Effects of Organizational Climate on Managerial Job Performance and Job Satisfaction", it was found that climate was influenced by both the overall organization and by subunits within the organization. Climate was fairly strongly related to subunit performance and to individual job satisfaction. There was some limited evidence for climate and individual needs interacting to influence performance and satisfaction.

Lawler, Hall, and Oldham (1974)[55]: in their article "Organizational Climate: Relationship to Organizational Structure, Process and Performance" come up with a model to explain the highly significant positive relationship between organizational climate factors and performance and job satisfaction. Two sets of relationships are especially noteworthy. The first of these is the highly significant relationship between organizational climate factors and the higher-order needs satisfaction items (i.e. esteem, autonomy and self-fulfillment). Climate is strongly related to scientists' feeling about the quality of their work experience. A second interesting and significant relationship is the one between climate factors and overall performance indices (i.e. new outside contracts, percentage of contracts meeting cost budget, number of reward contracts, etc).

Downey, Hellricgel, and Slocum (1975)[56]: In their article "Congruence Between Individual Needs, Organisational Climate, Job Satisfaction and Performance", explored how one could attempt to select those individuals whose needs are most congruent with the climate of the organization i.e., open, facilitative, who expert rewards for achievement people could seek individuals who desire to affiliate and tend toward sociability.

The organization's climate can be changed to more fully utilize the predispositions of managers and others.

Giri, and Pavan Kumar (2007)[57]: In their article "Impact of Organisational Climate on Job Satisfaction and Job Performance", was investigated impact of organizational climate among employees at three managerial levels from different Indian Organizations. It was found that organizational climate had a significant effect on job satisfaction and job performance. It was further observed that both organizational climate and job satisfaction differ significantly across the three levels of hierarchy, namely; top, middle and junior level managers.

Intervening Variable

In this category studies relating to organizational climate with leadership and stress are found.

(a) Studies on Leadership

Offeremann and Malamut (2002)[58]: In their article "When Leaders Harass: The Impact of Target Perceptions of Organizational Leadership and Climate on Harassment Reporting and Outcomes", examined the women who perceived that leaders made honest efforts to stop harassment, felt significantly freer to report harassment, were more satisfied with the complaint process, had greater commitment than did those viewing leaders as more harassment tolerant. Leaders are establishing an ethical organizational climate that reinforces formal harassment policies through actions.

(b) Studies on - Conflict and Stress

Dhillon (1991)[59]: In his article ,"Moderate Effects on the Occupational Stress –Job Satisfaction Relationship", made an attempt to investigate the effect of occupational stress on job satisfaction, and the moderator effects of age, education and hierarchy on this relationship.

Uma Bhowon (1999)[60]: Made an empirical study aiming at identifying the styles of handling interpersonal conflict and the impact of perceived organizational climate on the respondents' use of these styles with their superiors and subordinates. Altogether, 225 male executives representing 6 manufacturing concerns participated. Factor analysis results of the conflict handling style scale was confined to five factors namely, integrating, avoiding , compromising, obliging and dominating. Integrating, and dominating were the most and the least preferred styles for handling conflict with both targets. Power and independence oriented climates predicted the use of avoiding and integrating style in both contexts whereas achievement and independence climates determined the use of integrating, avoiding, and dominating style only with supervisors.

Brown and Ah-kion (2004)[61]: In their article "Organizational Climate and Stress A study of managers in Mauritius", examined the relationship of perceived Organizational Climate and Stress. Seven dimensions of stress and organizational climate were extracted through varimax rotated factor analysis, experience of inequity. Role overload, and inadequacy of role authority emerged as strong dimensions of stress, whereas job difficulty and lack of group cohesiveness were weak dimensions of stress. The significant relationship between dimensions of stress and climate indicate that employee's perceptions of the organization's structure and process determine stress experience.

Sanjay Kumar Singh (2005)[62]: studied, "Organizational Climate and Role Stress as Correlates of Journalistic Writing Attitude". The result of the study indicates that there is significant positive relationship between perceived internal environment of the organization and attitudes towards journalistic writing but significant negative relationship felt role stress with journalistic writing attitude among all the news paper reports.

The foregoing review of literature on organizational climate and job satisfaction identified three variables that are, dependent variable, independent variable and intervening variables. At suggest that's from time to time several investigations in India and abroad have been made and that there are many studies on banking sector, hospital, manufacturing sector, motivation, performance, conflict and stress. Almost all the studies agree that the three variables are positively correlated.

Different studies concluded different amounts of relationship between organizational climate and job satisfaction. Such a state of affairs will prompt any one to check the relationship for himself and this work is no exception.

STATEMENET OF THE PROBLEM

The organizational climate significantly differs from one organization to the other, one department to the other and even from one unit to the other, depending on various significant sub-factors constituting organizational climate. The organizational climate is the most important factor in job selection in an organization and it also affects the quantum of employees' turnover.

Job satisfaction refers to the result of various attitudes possessed by an employee. Further, workforce as a group tends to be inarticulate on the subject of job satisfaction and employees do not, in general, consider that they particularly got satisfied or dissatisfied. Hence, carefully interpreted individual attitudinal surveys, backed by in-depth individual interviews, probably provide the best index of job satisfaction.

Organizational climate is a composite of attitudes, beliefs and values that contributes to general feeling of satisfaction of people in an organization. It is a state of mind and spirit, affecting willingness to work. It is frequently referred to as being satisfaction and happiness of people working in an organisation's environment. It involves everything that makes a job a satisfying experience. A person with a favourable organizational climate and job satisfaction will have confidence in himself, in others and in his future. An individual with favourable organizational climate feels work is worth, doing well and that he is doing a good job. It also helps him to take minor irritation in his stride, and to work under pressure without blowing up.

Almost all the scientists unanimously agree regarding the importance of organizational climate and job satisfaction for these are the hall marks of several behavioural climates in the functioning of an organization. Therefore, organizational climate and job satisfaction have become the core areas for discussion, debate and research among all those who are working and striving for the cause of effective organizational functioning.

> How do these differences in organizational climate influence the job satisfaction level of TTD employees?

> What are the critical dimensions of organizational climate that affect job satisfaction?

These are a few questions. The present study is a humble attempt to analyse organizational climate and job satisfaction on selected parameters among TTD employees.

OBJECTIVES OF THE STUDY

The main objectives of the present study are to measure organizational climate and job satisfaction in select TTD employees.

1. To Study and analyze the dimensions of organizational climate of the employees selected for the present study

2. To identify the variations in perceptions on organizational climate among personal variables, and

3. To examine the overall job satisfaction with personal factors of the employees,

HYPOTHESES FORMULATED

The following hypotheses have been formulated and tested;

1. The perceptions on the dimensions of organizational climate differ among different groups based on personnel variables, and

2. Overall Job Satisfaction is not closely associated with the personal aspects of the Employees.

NEED FOR THE STUDY

There are a number of studies on the historical, religious, archaeological, sculptural, epi-graphical organization and, finances, employee – employer relations, personal and managerial aspects of the TTD and other temples in the country.

There has been no research work on the problems of organizational climate and job satisfaction in Tirumala Tirupati Devasthanams, a vast organization with twenty five departments and a large number of institutions, under its administrative control, wherein 11989 personnel in 180 cadres drawing different scales of pay and emoluments on a permanent basis. The administration of such a vast organization is in deed a stupendous task.

To maintain harmony among different cadres and the management of the large number of employees in TTD is a challenging task too.

The researcher has, therefore, felt a need to study the organization climate and job satisfaction in TTD with a view to exploring some ways and means of overcoming these problems, since there is a great paucity of research work on the problems of organizational climate and job satisfaction. That is why the researcher has undertaken this research work.

SIGNIFICANCE FOR THE STUDY

The researcher believes that this is the first research-based study on the theme of organizational climate and job satisfaction in TTD (Nay, for that matter, in any religious institution in India), with a research database. The researcher hopes that the various observations, findings, analysis, conclusions and suggestions made in the course of this work will be found useful and significant by those who are working in the area of organizational climate and job satisfaction, in any large scale, organization, particularly those related to endowments.

SAMPLE DESIGN

In the present research study, under statistical analysis, the researcher adopted suitable sampling technique namely 'Stratified Random Sampling with proportional allocation' for collecting the statistical data on Tirumala Tirupati Devasthanams (TTD) employees who were working in TTD during the period 2009-2010. Under this sampling scheme, all the employees of TTD have been divided into three strata namely, Professionals, Administrative Staff and Sub Staff.

Depending on the stratum size, under proportional allocation, three percent of total number of employees have been drawn randomly such that a random sample of 360 employees with a break –up of 36 Professionals, 109 Administrative Staff and 215 Sub-Staff, have been selected from TTD organisation.

Table 1. The following table shows the sampling frame for the present study.

Table 1: category – wise distribution of sample respondents			
S.No	Category of staff	Total number of employees	Number of Respondents
1	Professionals	1191	36
2	Administrative Staff	3625	109
3	Sub Staff	7173	215
	Total	11989	360

SCOPE OF THE STUDY

This study is exclusively made to understand, analyse and measure organizational climate and job satisfaction among the employees selected in Tirumala Tirupati Devasthanams.

METHOD OF DATA COLLECTION

The Present study is based on both secondary and primary data. Secondary data sources include electronic sources, published official reports on TTD, published books, research articles, magazines, professional journals and daily newspapers. To be specific, secondary data were culled out from websites of Tirumala Tirupathi

Devasthanams (TTD), Administrative Office and other places such as the Hindu religious and charitable endowments, Internet, theses and dissertations.

Primary data was generated canvassing the structured, pre-tested questionnaire to the sample respondents. The questionnaire has three sections from 'A' to 'C'. Section 'A' incorporates questions designed to collect data on demographics of sample respondents. Section 'B' is related to organization climate variables, Section 'C' is focused on Job Satisfaction.

DATA ANALYSIS (STATISTICAL TOOLS USED)

Primary data generated through structured questionnaire and secondary data collected from various official and non-official sources are statistically treated, using the wide array of statistical tools such as arithmetic mean, standard deviation, z-test, F- test, Chi – square test, correlation analysis, and factor analysis, graphics and figures are sparingly used to supplement the statistical treatment of data to draw meaningful inferences there from.

LIMITATIONS OF THE STUDY

The present study is undertaken within the limitations listed below:

❖ Apart from the factors / dimensions identified to analyze perception of organizational climate and job satisfaction, there could be yet many other factors that describe perception of organizational climate and job satisfaction directly and indirectly.

❖ There is unwillingness on the part of some respondents to spare time, due to work pressure. Some of the respondents showed a sort of uneasiness in explaining the feelings. Some respondents questioned; "what is the benefit of this?" the researcher has to convince the different types of respondents by telling about the academic value of the study. Despite this, it is suspected that there are some socially acceptable answers from some of the respondents. Through this study the researcher identified the relationship between:

❖ Perception of organizational climate and job satisfaction.
❖ Personal aspect of organizational climate and overall job satisfaction.

❖ It does not indicate cause – effect relationship

PLAN OF THE THESIS

The thesis is organized in to six chapters as follows

* ❖ **Chapter I:** A Theoretical frame work of Organizational Climate and Job Satisfaction-presents the theoretical framework of organizational climate and job satisfaction, in the changed organizational scenario.

* ❖ **Chapter II:** Review of Literature and Methodology-deals with Review of literature, Statement of the problem, Objectives of the study, Hypothesis formulated, Need and significance of the study, Database, various tools used for analysis of the data, including scope and limitations of the present study.

* ❖ **Chapter III:** Profile of Tirumala Tirupati Devasthanams-presents the Origin of TTD, and growth of TTD institutions, historical development, management of temples under kings and rulers, administration of temples under the state government.

* ❖ **Chapter IV:** Measurement of Organizational Climate-analyses the socio-demographic variables of the select respondents of organizational climate in TTD.

* ❖ **Chapter V:** Measurement of Job Satisfaction-analyses the socio-demographic variables of the select respondents having overall job satisfaction in TTD.

* ❖ **Chapter VI:** Findings, Conclusion and Suggestions-Summarizes the findings and offers suggestions for enhancing positive perception about organizational climate and job satisfaction among the employees in TTD.

REFERENCES

1. Roeth Lirsberger, F.J. and Diskson, W.J., **Management and the Worker**, Harvard University Press, Cambridge, 1939.

2. Frederisken N, "Some **Effects of Organisational Climate on Administrative Performance**, Research Memorandum, 1966 p-401.

3. Natarajan, R., "A Study on Organizational Climate and Teacher Morale", **Journal of Psychological Researches**, Vol. 45, No. 1, 2001, pp. 19 – 2 1.

4. Sumanlata," A Study of Educational Attainment as Function of School Organizational Climate", **Educational Research in Education and Psychology**, Vol. 10, No. 3, 4, 2005, pp. 100-103 .

5. Sharma R.D., and Jeevan Jyoti "Job Satisfaction Among School Teachers", **IIMB Management Review,** Vol.18, No.4 December, 2006 pp.349-363.

6. Lyon H.L., and Ivancevich J.M., "An Exploratory Investigation of Organizational Climate and Job Satisfaction in a Hospital" **Academy of Management Journal** Vol.17, No.4, 1974 pp.635-648.

7. Akhyilesh, K.B., and Pondey, S., "A Comparative Study of Organizational Climate in Two Banks", **Indian Journal of Industrial Relations**, Vol.21, No.4, April 1986, pp.456-461.

8. Jahan, R. and Haque, S., "Effects of Organisational Climate on Job Involvement, Job Satisfaction and Personality of Mid – level Managers", **The Bangladesh Journal of Psychology**, 1993, pp. 35-42.

9. Gani, A., and Farooq A. Sash., "Correlates of Organisational Climate in Banking Industry", **Indian Journal of Industrial Relations**, Vol.36, No.3, January 2001, pp. 301-322.

10. Sinha and Sharma "Union Attitude and Job Satisfaction in Indian workers". **Journal of Applied Psychology**, Vol.46, No.4, 1962, pp.247-251.

11. Guha T.N "Job Satisfaction Among Shoe Factory Workers", **Productivity,** Vol.VI, No.1, 1965 pp89-94.

12. Nataraj, C.L., and Hafeez, A., "A Study of Job Satisfaction Among Skilled Workers", **The Indian Journal of Social Work**, Vol. XXVI, No. 1, April 1965, pp. 9-12.

13. Peterson, R.B., "The Interaction of Technological Process Organizational Climate in Norwegian Firms", **Academy of Management Journal**, Vol. 18, June 1975, pp.288-299.

14. Pallavi Shash, "Need Importance and Need Fulfillment in Management Levels", **Indian Management**, May 1976, pp. 29-31, 45,

15. Klaleque, A., and Choudhury, N.,"Job Facets and Overall Job Satisfaction of Industrial Managers", **Indian Journal of Industrial Relations**, Vol. 20, No. 1, July 1984, pp. 55-64

16. Sharma, B.R., and Venkata Ratnam, C.S., "Organizational Climate and Supervisory – Management Relations in Ispat Nigam", **Indian Journal of Industrial Relations,** Vol. 23, No. 1, July, 1987. pp. 1-28.

17. Sebastian, M.P., and Bhargava, S., "Organizational Climate of Non- Profit Organization", **Productivity,** Vol. 43, No. 4, January-March, 2003, pp. 611-618.

18. Avinash Kumar Srivastav, "Organizational Climate in Public Sector: An Empirical Study", **Management & Change** Vol.10, No.2, 2006, pp.65-76.

19. Avinash Kumar Srivastav "Achievement Climate in Public Sector – A Cross Functional Study on Relationship with Stress and Coping" **IIMB Management Review**, Vol.19, No.4, December 2007, pp.415-425.

20. Bahadur katuwal and Gurprect Randhawa " Study of Job Satisfaction of Public and Private Sector Nepalese Textile Workers" **Indian Journal of Industrial Relations** Vol.43, No.23, October 2007, pp.239-253.

21. Chatterji, R., "Job Satisfaction", **Industrial Relations**, Vol. 12, 1960, pp. 262-264.

22. Singh, S.P., and Singh, A.P., "The Effect of Certain and Personal Factors on Job Satisfaction of Supervisors", **Psychological Studies**, Vol.25, 1961, pp. 127-132.

23. Ewen, R.B., "Some Determinants of Job Satisfaction: A Study of the Generality of Herzberg's Theory", **Journal of Applied Psychology**, Vol.48, N0.3, 1964, pp161-163.

24. Frank Friedlander "Job Characteristics as Satisfiers and Dissatisfiers", **Journal of Applied Psychology,** Vol.48, N0.6, 1964 pp.388-392.

25. Sarveswara Rao, G.V., and Ganapathi Rao, V., "A Study of Factors Contributing to Satisfaction and Importance of Industrial Personnel : A Test of the Two Factory Theory", **Indian Journal of Industrial Relations**, Vol. 9, No. 2, Oct 1973, pp. 233-262.

26. Sushila Singhal, "Measurement of Job Satisfaction on a Three – Dimensional Plane**", Indian Journal of Industrial Relations**, Vol. 9, No. 2, Oct 1973, pp. 263-279.

27. Hellriegel, D., and Slocum, J.W., "Organizational Climate: Measures, Research and Contingencies", **Academy of Management Journal**, Vol. 17, No. 2, June 1974, pp. 255-280.

28. Carrell, M.R., Elbert, N.F., "Some Personal and Organisational Determinants of Job Satisfaction of Postal Clerks", **Academy of Management Journal**, Vol. 17, No. 2, June 1974, pp. 368 – 372.

29. Schneider, B., "Organisational Climate: An Essay", **Personal Psychology**, Vol. 28, No. 4, winter 1975, pp. 447-479.

30. Schneider, B., and Snyder, R.A., "Some Relationship between Job Satisfaction and Organisational Climate", **Journal of Applied Psychology**, Vol. 60, No. 3, June 1975, pp. 318-328.

61

31. Payne, R.L., Fineman, S., and Wall, T.D., "Organisational Climate and Job Satisfaction: A Conceptual Synthesis", **Organisational Behaviour and Human Performance**, Vol. 16, No. 1, June 1976, pp. 45-62.

32. Muchinsky, P.M., "Organisational Communication: Relationship to Organisational Climate and Job Satisfaction", **Academy of Management Journal,** Vol. 20, No. 4, 1977, pp. 592-607.

33. Pramod Kumar, and Chandrakala Bora, "Job Satisfaction and Perceived Organisational Climate ", **The Indian Journal of Social Work**, Vol. XL, No. 1, April 1979. pp. 23-26.

34. Dwivedi, R.S., "Anatomy of Organizational Climate ", **Journal of the All India Management Association**, Vol. 18, No. 5, May 1979, pp.25-28, 36.

35. Poonam Bajaj., "Alienation as Related to Perception of Organizational Climate", **Indian Journal of Industrial Relations**, Vol. 17. No. 4, April 1982, pp563-572.

36. Arya, P.P., "Work Satisfaction and its Correlates", **Indian Journal of Industrial Relations**, Vol. 20, No. 1, July 1984, pp. 89-100.

37. Surya Kumar Srivastava "Relationship **Between Job Satisfaction and Organizational Climate**" Published Book, Print well Publishers, Jaipur (India) 1990, pp.320-228.

38. Dolke, A.M., "Personal – Personality, Job and Organisational Correlates of Work Identification", **The Indian Journal of Social Work**, Vol. LII, No. 4, Oct 1991, pp. 621-633.

39. Sayeed, O.B., "Organisational Effectiveness: Relationship with Job Satisfaction Facets", **Productivity**, Vol. 33, No. 3, October- December, 1992. pp. 422-429.

40. Rama Devi, V., "**Faculty Job Satisfaction and their views on Management – Study of two Universities in Andhra Pradesh**" unpublished Ph.D. thesis in Commerce, submitted to S.K.University, Anantapur.

41. Taylor. H, "The Differences between Exercisers and Non-exercisers on Work Related Variables", **International Journal of Stress Management**, Vol. 7, 2000, pp.307-309.

42. Chakrapani, D., **"Job Satisfaction Among Employees of Select Manufacturing Units in Cuddapah, Andhra Pradesh"**, Unpublished Ph.D. thesis in Commerce, submitted to S.V.University, Tirupati. 2001.

43. Sinha, B.P., and Gupta, p., et.al "Societal Beliefs, Organizational Climate, and Managers' Self- Perceptions", **Vikalpa**, Vol. 26, No. 1, January-March 2001, pp. 33-47.

44. Sharma, V.c., Gaur, A.K., Srivastava, S.K., and Pandey, R.S., "Job Satisfaction of Women Workers", **The Indian Journal of Commerce**, Vol.54, No.4, Oct.-Dec. 2001, pp. 157-163.

45. Antony Joseph "Job Ssatisfaction Among Transport Employees", **Journal of Psychological Researches,** Vol.45, No.2, 2001, pp.58-61.

46. Malik, K., and Goyal, D.P., "Organizational Environment and Information System", **Vikalpa,** Vol. 28, No. 1, January- March 2003, pp.61-74.

47. Bose, S., and Agarwal, M., "Organizational Work Climate and Perceived 'Procedural Fairness' of Human Resource Practices", **Psychological Studies**, Vol. 50, No. 2, and 3, April and July 2005, pp. 243- 249.

48. Sailaja Rani **"Job Satisfaction Among Bank Employees in Chittoor District of A.P."** Thesis Submitted to S.V.University, Tirupati, March. 2006.

49. Srimannarayana. M., "Human Resource Development Climate in Dubai Organizations" **Indian Journal of Industrial Relations**, Vol. 43, No.1, July 2007, pp. 1 – 12.

50. A P Sing and Sadhana Singh "Effects of Stress and Work Culture on Job Satisfaction" **The Icfai University Journal of Organizational Behaviour**, Vol. VIII, No.2, Aprial 2009, pp- 52-62.

51. Sharma, B.R., "Employee Motivation and Employer –Employee Relations In India", **Indian Management**, June 1983 pp. 8-14.

52. Archana Tarabadkar and Rehana Ghadially "Achievement Motivation and Job Satisfaction", **Productivity,** Vol. XXVI, No.3 1985, pp.231-237.

53. Srivastava, A.K., "Motivation and Perception of Organizational Climate" **Productivity,** Vol. XXXVI, N.1, 1985, pp.55-58.

54. Pritchard R.D., and Karasick B.W., "The Effects of Organizational Climate on Managerial Job Performance and Job Satisfaction", **Organizational Behaviour and Human Performance,** Vol.9, No.1, February, 1973,   pp.126-146.

55. Lawler, E.E., Hall, D.T., and Oldham, G.R., "Organizational Climate: Relationship to Organizational Structure, Process and Performance", **Organizational Behaviour and Human Performance**, Vol. 11, No.1 Feb 1974, pp. 139-155.

56. Downey, H.K., Hellricgel, D., and Slocum, J.W., "Congruence Between Individual Needs, Organisational Climate, Job Satisfaction and Performance", **Academy of Management Journal**, Vol. 18, No. 1, March 1975, pp. 149-155.

57. Giri, V.N., and Pavan Kumar, B., "Impact of Organisational Climate on Job Satisfaction and Job Performance", **National Academy of Psychology**, India, Vol. 52, No.2, 2007, pp. 131-133.

58. Offeremann, L.R., and Malamut, A.B., "When Leaders Harass: The Impact of Target Perceptions of Organizational Leadership and Climate on Harassment Reporting and Outcomes", **Journal of Applied Psychology**, Vol.87, No. 5, pp. 885-893.

59. Dhillion, P.K., "Moderate Effects on the Occupational Stress –Job Satisfaction Relationship", **Productivity,** Vol. 31, No. 4, January – March, 1991, pp.584-590.

60. Uma Bhowon., "Perceived Organisational Climate and Interpersonal Conflict Handling Strategies", **Indian Journal of Industrial Relations**, Vol.35, No.1, July 1999, pp. 43-54.

61. Bhowon, U., and Ah-kion, J., "Organizational Climate and Stress- A study of Managers in Mauritius", **Psychological Studies**, Vol. 49, No. 1, January 2004, pp. 45-51.

62. Sanjay Kumar Singh, " Organizational Climate and Role Stress as Correlates of Journalistic Writing Attitude", **Indian Journal of Industrial Relations**, Vol. 41, No. 2, October 2005, pp. 206- 217.

Chapter - III

PROFILE OF TIRUMALA TIRUPATI DEVASTHANAMS

An attempt is made in this chapter to study the historical development of the T.T.D. ad-ministration from the earliest times unto the period of the British rule, history of the management of the T.T.D. under the various acts of the State Government, Sudarsanam token system, Social Activities, Educational Activities, Religious Activities, Sevas and **Endowment Scheme.**

INTRODUCTION

The Lord of Tirumala is the all-pervading Lord of the Universe.A large number of devotees-daily 50,000 on an average, visit the sacred shrine of Lord Venkateswara to pay their homage to Him.Tirumala Tirupati Devasthanams have in turn, dedicated themselves to these devotees by providing facilities for darshan, accommodation as well as for sevas. The chief aim of the Devasthanams has always been to improve these facilities for making the pilgrimage a spiritual experience.

HISTORICAL DEVELOPMENT OF THE T.T.D ADMINISTRATION

Indian temples are rich in architecture and sculpture and have an important place in the cultural and socio-economic development of the people.

South India is the land of temples and monuments for preserving and propagating our heritage, culture and civilization[1]. The temples of Tirumala and Tirupati are the most prominent among the South Indian temples. They have been well known from ancient times.

According to the legends Tirumala is the most sacred place on the earth. Pilgrims from all over the world visit this shrine for worshipping "Lord Venkateswara" in millions all through the year. It is situated at a height of 2,980 feet above the sea level and enjoys salubrious and invigorating climate[2]. It is the oldest religious institution and in the world having a record of unbroken worship carried over a span of 1300 years.

In the Eastern Ghats in Chittoor District, Andhra Pradesh, the Tirumala hill range has seven principal peaks. The temple stands on "Seshachalam". The other hills are called Anjanadri, Garudadri, Venkatadri, Narayanadri, Vrishanbadri and Niladri. There is a firm belief that it is not an installed image but Lord Vishnu Himself took the shape i.e. "Swayambhoo", to preside over the kaliyuga[3].

The Lord is popularly called as "Yedu Kondala Vada" in the state of Andhra Pradesh and "Srinivasa Perumal" in the adjoining Tamil Nadu. In the North India Lord Venkatesware is famous as "Balaji". The day in Tirumala temple commences with the "Suprabhatham" – a pre – dawn seva meant to awaken the Lord from His "Yoga Nidhra". The pundits recite the Suprabhatha verses composed by a 15th century composer, "Prathevadhe Bhayankara Mannan".

One of the important festivals celebrated in Tirumala is "Brahmotsavam". The belief is the Lord Brahma Himself comes to Tirumala during Brahmotsavam and performs the festival. Tirumala – the "Kaliyuga Vaikuntam" goes gay, adds glitter in all its splendour during the annual Brahmotsavam, normally held during the month of October every year[4].

There are four main pathways leading to Tirumala, two well – laid asphalt motorable Ghat roads and two sopanamargas (flight of steps). The vehicles coming down from the hills use the old ghat road. It was laid in 1944 and its length is about 19 Kms. And the vehicles going up the hills use the second ghat road, which was opened in 1974, with its length about 20 Kms. These ghat roads facilitate easy and comfortable transportation to Tirumala. The bus transport, which was originally run by the T.T.D., was handed over to the Andhra Pradesh State Road Transport Corporation on 10-8-1975. There is an ancient soponamarga about 11 Kms in length from the foot of hills i.e. from Alipiri used by the pilgrims who come up hills on foot. There is yet another short but stiffer route from Chandhragiri side which is about 6 Kms, only from the foot of the hills. These footpaths are re-laid by fixing cut-stone slabs all through the length of the route for enabling the pilgrims to go on foot [5].

Tirupati on the plains is itself a pilgrimage center, as the temple of Sri Padmavathi i.e.Alivelumanga, the consort of the Lord, is situated in Tiruchanoor about 5 Kms from Tirupati and Sri Kalyana Venkateswara Swamy Temple at

Srinivasa Mangapuram about 10 Kms from Tirupati. Sri Govindaraja Temple is in the center of Tirupati town. Sri Kapileswara Temple is situated one and half Kms to the North of Tirupati town on the eastern bank of Kapilatheeram tank. Sri Kodandarama Swamy temple is located in the heart of the town[6].

All the temples at Tirumala and Tirupati are sacred for all Hindus. With implicit faith, people turn to Lord Venkateswara for help in their Critical situations, or to realize their desires and expectations.

Lord Vishnu Himself has descended from His celestial height to Tirumala hills to grace the people of Kaliyuga and shower on them all blessing they seek. The Vaishnava Alwars song in praise of the Lord, describing Him as "Self manifestation of Vishnu", "Destroyer of sins", and "Giver of all Boons[7]".

MANAGEMENT OF TEMPLES UNDER KINGS AND RULERS

It was during the eight century that the Alwars recognized Tirupati temples as a temple shrine. The praise pf the Lord was a running point in the history of Tirumala temple.

The earliest political history of this Vengadam[8] was connected with Satavahanas who were the feudatories of Mauryan Dynasty. After the Satavahanas, Vengadam was ruled by a local chieftain, by name, "pulli[9]". According to the local sources he was the person who arranged poojas of Lord Venkatesware in the temple.

In India, religious and charitable institutions came under the protection and patronage of ruling kings. The temples of Tirumala and Tirupati were directly under the successive control of the kings and Emperors of different regimes. There are numerous inscriptions referring to the receipt of a stream of royal benefictions by the Tirumala temple from 1530 A.D. down to 1830 A.D.[10]

PALLAVA PERIOD (260 – 900 A.D.)

The age of Pallavas constitutes the first important landmark in the history of Thondamandalam and Tirumala-Tirupati region. After Satavahanas, the Pallavas of

Kanchi established their authority over this region. The actual history of Tirumala temple starts only with the Pallavas who constructed the present temple complex of Tirumala and covered the Sikhara with Gold plates[11].

The Pallava kings appeared to be the earliest donors to the Lord's temple and undertook the repairs of the temple and Soponamarga i.e. the foot pathway.

During the early Pallava period there was a sabha at Tiruchanoor (5 Km from the Tirupati). This sabha was looking after political, administrative and religious functions on behalf of the king.

CHOLA PERIOD (900 – 1250 A.D.)

After the Pallavas the Cholas, of Tanjore extended royal patronage to these temples. There are 31 inscriptions belonging to the various rulers of the Chola dynasty which record the gifts made to the temples[12]

It between the Pallavas and Cholas the Pandyas also patronized the temple of Lord Venkateswara and added some structures to the temple complex.

VIJAYANAGARA PERIOD (1336 – 1672 A.D.)

Vijayanagara Rulers ruled South India from 1336 – 1672 A.D. with their fortunes fluctuating from time to time. Lord Venkateswara was the patron deity of these monarchs. Sri Krishnadevaraya was a great devotee of Lord Venkateswara at Tirumala and Lord Siva at Sri Kalahasti. His first visit to the temple was reported to be on 10th February 1513. In all he made seven visits to Tirumala accompanied by his two queens, Tirumaladavi and Chinnadevi.

They offered several gifts and endowments to the Lord of the Seven Hills. He presented a Gold crown set with precious gems, and Goad plates for lighting camphor lights. The gilding of Divya – Vimanam with Gold was completed by 1518 A.D. by Sri Krishnadevaraya.

During the period there was one officer called "Sthanattar" or trustee who received gifts and endowments offered to the temple[13]. Sri Krishnadevaraya appointed a number of temple administrators to carry out the daily offerings and poojas to the

70

Lord. The statues of Sri Krishnadavaraya and his consorts Tirumaladevi and Chinnadevi were installed in Tirumala temple to commemorate their services to the Lord Seven hills.

MUSLIM RULE (1650-1800 A.D.)

By 1650 A.D. South India came under the Muslim rule. Lala Khermaram, the Rajput General of Nawab Sadat-ulla-Khan (1710-1732) acted as a protector of the Tirumala temple[14].

The Tirumala Tirupati region was conquered by the Sultans of Golkonda by about the middle of the 17th century and remained under the Muslim rule for about a century and a half.

The rulers of Mysore, namely Hyderali and his son Tippu Sultan, extended their patronage to the Tirumala temple. From 1746 to 1751 A.D. the Tirumala temple came under the control of French. Azim-U-Doula, Nawab of Arcot, surrendered the Karnataka region to the British East India Company in 1801. As a result Tirumala and Tirupati came under the control of East India Company[15].

EAST INDIA COMPANY (1801 – 1843 A.D.)

The East India Company took over the management of the temples at Tirumala and Tirupati from the Nawab of Arcot in 1801. These temples were under the direct control of the Company from 1801 to 1843[16].

With the advent of British, the management passed on to the hands of the East India Company. Mr. M.G. Strallon, then collector of North Arcot District (in 1803), reported, after the investigation and enquiries, to the Board of Revenue on 31-1-1803 detailing the sources of Revenue of the said temples.

Subsequently, under the regulation VII of 1817 of the Madras Government, the management of the temples was carried on under the control of the Board of Revenue through the collector of North Arcot District.

A code of departmental instructions for the proper management of Tirumala Tirupati Devasthanams was managed according to the rules in "Bruce-Code"[17].

MAHANTS OF HATHEERAMJI MUTT (1843 – 1933 A.D.)

The Mahant of the Hatheeramji Mutt[18] took over the administration as "Vicharana Kartha" executing "Kararunama" on 16-7-1843[19]. In 1842 some members in the British Parliament demanded that the British Government in India should observe a strict policy of non-intervention in religious matters[20]. Thus this administration of Tirumala Tirupati temples was handed over to the Mahant.

During the Mahant Management the source of income of these temples gradually increased while the period of the Mahant provided clean and efficient administration. But in course of time their administration proved to be ineffective, misused the temple funds and misappropriated the temple property.

ADMINISTRATION OF TEMPLES UNDER THE STATE GOVERNMENT

The Mahants were incharge of the management of the Tirumala Tirupati Devasthanams till 1933. In order to prevent the misuse of temple funds and misappropriation of the temple property, the Tirumala Tirupati Devasthanams Act of 1932 was passed by the Government of Madras.

By the Madras Act of 1933 the management of the Tirumala Tirupati Devasthanams was transferred and vested in "Tirumala Tirupati Devasthanams Committee". The committee was constituted as a corporate body having perpetual succession and common seal and it carried on the administration through a Commissioner appointed by the government. The said 1933 Act was replaced by an enactment in 1951 and the administration of T.T.D. was entrusted to a Board of Trustees. The State Government also appointed an Executive Officer. After the formation of Andhra Pradesh State in 1953 the Andhra Government adopted the said Act of 1951. Subsequently, the Government of Andhra Pradesh amended it by a comprehensive enactment, namely "The A.P. Charitable and Hindu Religious Institutions Act 1966(Act No of 1966)"which came into force on 26-1-1967.Chapter XIV there of dealt with the administration of the Tirumala Tirupati Devasthanams. Subject to the other general provisions of the Act under the said Act of 1966, the administration was under the control of the Commissioner of Endowments, A.P. The legislature had enacted the T.T.D. Act No. of 1979 which came into force from 18-5-1979. The administration of T.T.D. was thus run according to the Act 20 / 1979 and the rules made there under.

Subsequently, the Government of Andhra Pradesh appointed a Commissioner under the Chairmanship of a retired, judge justice, Sri Challa Kondaiah with an objective of studying the entire system of the administration of the Hindu Religious, Charitable Endowments and Institutions in the State of Andhra Pradesh. Basing on its report and the recommendations made by the Commission in its report the Government of Andhra Pradesh issued an enactment which was published as the " Andhra Pradesh Charitable and Hindu Religious Institutions and Endowments Act 1987" (Act 30 / 1987). The act came into force with effect from 23rd May 1987. Under this Act the Tirumala Tirupati Davasthanams formed an integral part of entire lot of the Hindu Religious Institutions and Endowments in the State of Andhra Pradesh. However, a separate chapter (Chapter – XIV) was prescribed for TTD. Also it is specified in the act that the other provisions of this Act shall be subject to the provisions of the Chapter - XIV and apply to the TTD as a whole and to every specific Endowment attached either to TTD as a whole or to any temple or institution there of [21].

HIGHLIGHTS OF ADMINISTRATION SET-UP

The act 30/87 came into force on 23-5-1987. Prior to the said date, the TTD Act 20/1979 governed the T.T.D. The salient features of the Act 30/1987 are as follows.

1. The administration of the T.T.D. vests with the Board of Trustees.
2. The Chief Administrative Officer of the T.T.D. is the Executive Officer. He is also given the general powers to carry out the provisions of the Act, subject to the control of the Board.
3. The Board of Trustees under section 97(VII) and the Executive Officer under section 109 (2) may delegate their powers to the Executive Officer and to the subordinate officers respectively.

A committee called the T.T.D. Management Committee has to be appointed by the Government, which is vested with the powers to discharge the functions of the T.T.D. Board of Trustee, so far as the administration of the T.T.D. is concerned[22]

THE EXECUTIVE OFFICER

The executive officer of T.T.D. shall be appointed by the Government from the rank of a District Collector or a post not lower in rank than that of a District Collector in any other service in the state government[23.] He holds office for a term of three years and is eligible for re-appointment for another term[24].

Source of income

The temple of Venkateswara is one of the largest income fetching shrines in India. It is the cult of Venkateswara, which has played an important role in bringing vast amounts of revenue to the temple.

The sources of income are the deposits by devotees in the offertorium (holy gift box) popularly know as 'hundi', the receipts obtained with reference to the paid service popularly known as 'Arjita Seva', the special entrance fee, charged for providing facilities in the choultries, the toll-gate collection at the foot of the hills, the sale of sacred foods (Prasadam), the sale of gold dollars containing the image of the deity, the canteen sales, the sale of human hair, and the sale of TTD publications.

GENERAL FACILITIES AT TIRUMALA

Many pilgrims walk up the hills as a part of their vow to the Lord. The T.T.D. has provided the following facilities to them

- Transportation of luggage free of charge to Tirumala.The pilgrims can deposit their luggage at any of the choultries in Tirupati, or at the toll gate at Alipiri, against a token and take delivery of the luggage at the central reception office counter at Tirumala.
- Provision for cooking at Galigopuram, Chittiyekkudu, and Mamanduru Mitta, Narasimhaswami temple, Mokallamitta and other places.

- Availability of drinking water all along the footpath.
- Facility of canteen runs under hygienic conditions by the voluntary organisation "ISKCON" at Mamanduru Mitta (Seventh mile).
- Availability of toilets.
- Provision of sunshade at important points for taking rest.
- Arrangements for patrol by Security guards, Gurkhas and Police all along the road throughout day and night to prevent unwary pilgrims from being cheated or robbed by unscrupulous elements.
- Relay of religious programmes through local broadcasting system.

SUDARSANAM / BIOMETRIC TOKENS SYSTEM

Pilgrims were experiencing difficulties in waiting in the long queue lines for hours and days together along with children and old people. In order to minimize waiting time of the devotees in the queue compartments and reduce their hardship, Sudarsan/Biometrics token was introduced by the TTD. The pilgrims can now enter Vaikuntam Queue Complex-1 at the given date and time and complete Srivari darshan within two hours after entering the queue line.

WHAT IS SUDARSANAM

'Sudarsanam', a bar coded wristband token, is tied to the right hand wrist. It gives reporting time and date of Srivari darshan to the pilgrims. Now wristband token is replaced with biometrics token, where thumb impression of the pilgrim along with digital photo is taken and a token is given with reporting date and time of Srivari darshan. Pilgrim's thumb impression will be verified at Vaikuntam Queue Complex-1.In case, it does not tally with the thumb impression given at the counter, the pilgrim will not be allowed for darshan. Biometrics tokens are also issued for free and paid darshan in all counters located at tirumala and Tirupati. Free Sudarsanam tokens are available at Tirupati only.

PRECAUTIONS TO BE TAKEN

Sudarsanam/biometrics tokens are issued at the TTD counter only. These tokens are not available elsewhere in Tirumala or Tirupati.

Tokens are issued for each and every pilgrim and not for groups. Children, who are below 12 years, need not wear Sudarsanam tokens. They are allowed free for darshan.

The pilgrims are advised not to trust dalalies or touts. For further information, they are asked contact your nearest 'TTD Information Centre' for help and assistance.

Special Darshan for Physically disabled and Aged

This special darshan is arranged for the physically disabled and the aged, the infants along with parents through a separate gate at the Maha Dwaram, the main temple entrance. If necessary, such pilgrims can be accompanied by an attendant.

Social Service

TTD has taken many social service initiatives in areas like education, medical treatment, and rehabilitation of the physically challenged and economically backward. It also provides aid to authors and subsidised equipment to other temples.

- ❖ Social Activities
- ❖ Educational Activities
- ❖ Religious Activities
- ❖ Publications
- ❖ Literary Research.

Social Activities

- Balaji Institute of Surgery, Research and Rehabilitation for the Disabled
- Sri Venkateswara Poor Home
- Sri Venkateswara Bala Mandir
- Sri Venkateswara Institute of Medical Sciences
- Sri Venkateswara School for the Deaf
- Sri Venkateswara Training Centre for the Handicapped
- Conservation of Water and Forests - Haritha Project

Rituals: Tirupati Devasthanams (TTD) of Tirumala Tirupati, one of the Greatest Temples in INDIA is doing great social service, work, be it in medical field like treating everyone irrespective of caste, creed or religion or in helping people who cannot bear the expenses by giving free treatment. It is maintaining a poor home, a home for treatment of leprosy patients, a bala mandir for orphans and destitutes, to feed and educate them and offers boarding and lodging. TTD has a training centre for the handicapped people and a school for the deaf. It also supllies free food for people. Apart from undertaking research and development in the medical fields, it is also working to conserve underground water and rain water. It has developed many programmes to do so. It is planting saplings and developing forests to improve the rain.

Educational Activities

In 1876, when the temple administration was under the control of the Mahant of Hathiramjee Mutt, an educational institution called the Hindu High School was founded in Vellore (North Arcot District, Tamilnadu). In 1886, another Hindu High School was established in Tirupati. After TTD came into being, the names of both schools were changed to SV High School.

Today, TTD runs separate degree colleges, junior colleges and high schools for boys and girls, in and around Tirupati. It also runs a degree college in New Delhi. With a view to propagate and popularise Sanskrit and other ancient languages, TTD has established the Sri Venkateswara Oriental High School and Sri Venkateswara Oriental College at Tirupati, and the SVVVS College at Hyderabad. TTD also runs a Music and Dance college to impart education in ancient Indian Arts. TTD maintains a Vedapatasala and Sculpture Training Centre. TTD has also founded an Ayurveda College, to train students in India's age-old medical system.

Professional Colleges
- S.V.Institute of Traditional Sculpture & Architecture, Tirupati
- SV Polytechnic for the Physically Challenged (SVPPC), Tirupati
- SV Ayurvedic College, Tirupati
- SPW Polytechnic, Tirupati
- SV Yoga Institute, Tirupati

- SV College of Music and Dance, Tirupati

Oriental Colleges

- SV Oriental College, Tirupati
- SVVVS College, Secunderabad

Degree Colleges

- SV College, New Delhi
- SV Arts college, Tirupati
- SPW College, Tirupati
- Sri Govindaraja Swami Arts College, Tirupati.

Junior Colleges

- SV Junior College, Tirupati
- SPW Junior College, Tirupati

High Schools

- SV Higher Secondary School, Vellore
- SV High School, Tirupati
- SP Girls High School, Tirupati
- SGS High School, Tirupati
- SV Oriental High School, Tirupati
- SKRS (EM) High School, Tirupati
- SV High School, Tirumala

Elementary Schools

- SV Elementary School, Tirupati
- SKS Elementary School, Thatithopu
- SV Elementary School, Tirumala
- SV Elementary School, Tirumala

Religious Activities

Tirumala Tirupati Devasthanams (TTD) is also taking up religious activities and spreading the message of Hindu Dharma. Its main motto is "Follow and Save Dharma and Dharma will save you."

- Annamacharya Project
- Dasa Sahitya Project

- Alwar Divya Prabhanda Project
- Sri Venkateswara Veda Recording Project
- Sri Venkateswara Video Audio Recording Project
- Tarigonda Vengamamba Project
- Haritha Project
- Temple Renovation and Reconstruction
- Sriman Veturi Prabhakara Sastry Vangmaya Peetam

Sri Tallapaka Annamacharya was a saint composer in the fifteenth century, who hailed from the Tallapaka village, in the Rajampet mandal of Cuddapah district, Andhra Pradesh, India. Annamacharya was the very first vaggeyakara (composer) in Telugu and established a tradition that was later followed by a number of saint composers like Tyagaiah and Kshetraiah. Annamacharya composed 32,000 keertanas (devotional songs) in praise of Lord. The project functions through three wings - Music, Research and Publications, and Recording.

The Dasa Sahitya Project propagates and popularises the literature of the saint composers of Karnataka, popularly known as Karnataka Haridasas, who enriched Kannada religious literature with their hymns. Karnataka Haridasas who brought the esoteric Vedas, Upanishads and Puranas within the reach of the common man in lyrical form in simple Kannada, composed thousands of hymns in praise of Lord Sri Venkateswara, thus preaching devotion of God.

SV Central Library and Research Centre

Sri Venkateswara Central Library and Research Centre (SVCLRC) was established by TTD in 1993. It houses approximately 40,000 volumes of rare and valuable books, mainly on religion and philosophy.

Sevas

Arjitha Seva means performing seva to the Lord on payment of a fee to the temple. Tirumala Tirupati Devasthanams oversee the worship of the Lord and His finances. There are three kinds of Sevas: Daily Seva, Weekly Seva and Annual Seva.

Daily Sevas

Suprabhatam

'Suprabhatam' is the first and foremost seva at Tirumala; Suprabhatam signifies the ritual performed at Sayana Mandapam to wake up the Lord from His celestial sleep, amidst chanting of the hymns. Every day, in the early hours, acharyapurushas sing the hymns beginning with 'Kausalya Supraja Rama' while a descendant of Tallapaka Annamacharya recites Annamayya's matin songs. 'Suprabhatam' hymn consist of Suprabhatam, Stotram, Prapattithe and Mangalasanam composed by Prativadi Bhayankara Annan, a disciple of the celebrated Vaishnava preceptor, Manavala Mamuni.

Devotees present at the time of suprabhatham can have the suprabhatha darshana, also called visvarupa darsanam.

Thomala Seva

The presiding deity of Lord Srinivasa, festival deities and other deities are exquisitely decorated with floral and tulasi garlands during this seva. 'Thomala' denotes the decoration of the deities with garlands. The grihasthas who have paid the requisite amount can have darshan of the Lord during Thomala seva. However, the priests decorate the main deity of Lord Venkateswara with flowers brought by Ekangi or flowers specially brought from Flower room by Jeeyangar.

The deity is then adorned with the flowers while the mantra pushpam is recited in the sayanamandapam.

Sahasranama Archanantara

Archana to the main deity, Lord Venkateswara, is performed amidst chanting of one thousand names of the Lord. This occurs immediately after 'Suprabhatam' and Thomala seva.

Kalyanotsavam

Srivari Kalyanotsavam is performed to the utsava murti of the Lord Sri Malayappa swami and His consorts, Sridevi and Bhudevi, in the marriage hall in the Sampangi Pradakshinam. References to this Seva conducted on special occasions are found in the inscriptions of the 15th century. The wedding ceremony is held amidst recitation of the Vedic mantras and pronouncing the family pedigree of the brides and bridegroom. The idols of the Lord and His brides face each other with a screen in between. They are allowed to see each other only at the appropriate auspicious moment when the screen is removed. The priests perform homas. A purohit conducts the marriage and an archaka is consecrated to perform other rituals on behalf of the bridegroom. This seva is not performed on important festivals like Srivari Brahmotsavam, Pavitrotsavam, Pushpayagam etc. and on the days of solar and lunar eclipses. The grihasthas who participate in the seva are given prasadams and clothes. The duration of the seva is about one hour.

Arjitha Brahmotsavam

The Brahmotsavam is performed daily in an abridged manner in the vaibhavotsava Mantapam, opposite Srivari Temple. Sri Malayappa Swami with His two consorts is worshipped with Vedic mantras and rituals and mounted on three vahanams- golden Peddasesha Vahanam, silver Garuda Vahanam and silver Hanumantha Vahanam and offered worship. This seva is conducted only after the Kalyanotsavam.

Dolotsavam (Unjal Seva)

Sri Malayappaswami, Sridevi and Bhudevi are seated in an unjal (Swing) in the Aina Mahal (Addala Mantapam) opposite Ranganayaka mantapam. It is enchanting to see the gorgeous reflections of the Lord's glorious presence everywhere. The deities are swung to the accompaniment of Veda parayanam and mangalavadyam.

Arjita Vasanthotsavam

This seva is conducted in the Vaibhavotsava Mantapam as an arjitam. The seva is offered to Sri Malayappa swami and His consorts daily. Perfumeries are lavishly used to create an ethereal atmosphere. The Veda pandit chants Purusha suktam, Sri suktam and other Vedic hymns. Abhishekam is done to the Lord and His consorts with sacred water. Later, abhishekam is performed with milk, curd, honey and turmeric. Finally, sandal paste is applied to Sri Malayappa Swami and consorts. The duration of the seva is about one hour.

Sahasra Deepalankarana Seva

Every day in the evening, at 5:30 p.m. Sahasra deepalankarana seva is performed in the Unjal mantapam located on the southeastern corner of the Srivari Temple.Sri Malayappa swami along with Sridevi and Bhudevi is taken out in procession to the mantapa, where one thousand wick lamps are lit. In the midst of Vedic chanting and singing of Annamaya Sankirtanas, the Lord, seated on an unjal, is rocked gently.

Ekanta Seva

Ekanta Seva is the last ritual among the daily sevas. Sarvadarsanam comes to a close with Ekanta Seva. Sri Bhoga Srinivasa Murthi, the silver image of the main deity is seated in the Sayana Mantapam in a golden cot. During Ekanta seva, a descendant of Annamacharya sings lullabies to put the Lord to sleep. This seva is also known as panupu seva. Tarigonda Vengamamba's harati (in a plate inlaid with one of the dasavataras on each day with pearls) is offered to the Lord. Bhoga Srinivasa occupies the cot for eleven months in a year and in the twelfth month of Dhanurmasa (Margali) Sri Krishna is put to sleep.

Weekly Sevas

Visesha Puja (On Mondays)

This seva was first introduced in srivari temple on April 8, 1991. The seva takes place on every Monday morning. Sri Malayappa Swami and His consorts are taken to kalyanamandaam and worship is offered to them with homas and tirumanjanam as per vaikhanasa agama.

Ashtadala - Pada Padmaaradhana (On Tuesdays)

This seva is conducted after the second bell. This ritual was first introduced in Srivari Temple in 1984 when a Muslim devotee offered Lord Srinivasa 108 gold lotuses. The archaka commences the puja by offering dhupa and dipa to the main deity. Then he recites the Dvadasa names of the Lord. While uttering each name of the Lord, one golden lotus is offered at the feet of the lord. On completion of the archana for the mula murti, archana is offered for Goddesses Lakshmi and Padmavati. Later. Ratha arati is offered first, followed by ordinary arati.

Sahasra Kalasabhishekam (on Wednesdays)

Every Wednesday before sarva darsanam, sahasra kakasabhishdka is performed for bhoga srinivasa with pure water in perfumed One thousand silver vessels.

Tiruppavada Seva (On Thursdays)

Every Thursday after sattumari, Tiruppavada seva takes place in Tirumamani mantapam. This service consists of cooking a large quantity of rice as pulihora and offering it to the Lord along with other sweet preparations such as payasam, laddu, jilebi, thenthola, appam etc. The cooked rice is heaped up in mukha mantapam to take definite customary primidal trapezoid shape and the delicacies are deposited thereon with coconuts, flowers, sandal paste, kumkum, deepam and are offered to the Lord with appropriate mantras.

Abhishekam (On Fridays)

Abhishekam to the lord is performed in the early morning every Friday. Camphor, saffron and milk are used for giving a sacred bath to the lord.

After chanting of the Vedic mantras and prabandham, abishekam is performed to the gold image of Sri Lakshmi, which hangs in a gold chain in the chest amidst the chanting of sri suktam. The lord is then dressed in a pitambaram and adorned with valuable ornaments.

Nijapada darsanam

Every Friday, after abhishekam, devotees are allowed for nijapada darsanam. They can worship the load's holy feet without any frills during this darsan. The lord's feet will be decorated with ornaments on other occasions.

Periodical Sevas
Float festival

This was instituted by Saluva Narasimha in the sixteenth century. The festival is celebrated for five days. On the first day, lord Krishna in the Navanita Nritya pose is worshipped. On the second day, Sri Rama is seated on the float and offered the worship. On third to fifth day Sri Malayappaswami along with Sridevi and Bhudevi is worshipped .The utsava deities are daily decorated and taken in procession in the Pushkarini on a beautifully decorated float.

Vasanthotsavam

It is a three - day festival conducted at Tirumala on the days of Tryodasi, Chaturdasi and Pournami in the month of chitra (March / April). On all the days, Sri Malayappaswami and His Consorts are taken round in procession and brought to the Vaibhavotsava mantapam, where Abhishekam is performed. On the Third day, Sri Rama with Sita, Lakshmana and Anjaneya and Sri Krishna with Rukmini and Satyabhama are also taken out in procession and brought to the Vaibhavotsava mantapam.

Teppotsavam

Every year, during Phalguna Pournami, this festival is celebrated on a grand scale in the Swami Pushkarini for five days. On the first day, Lord Rama with Sita and Lakshmana is offered worship. On the second day, Sri krishna and Rukmini are offered puja. During the remaining three days beginning with Trayodasi and ending with Pournami, Sri Malayappa Swami, along with Sridevi and Bhudevi, is worshipped. The utsava murtis are impressively decorated on these days and taken on a beautiful float specially erected in the Pushkarini.

Abhideyaka Abhishekam

This ritual, also called jyeshtabhishekam is performed in the month of jyeshta for three days. This is held in the kalyanamandaam in a solemn manner.

The festival is meant is for proper protection and preservation of the utsava idols through various pujas and mantras. On the first day, the golden idol of the lord is removed and abhishekam and snapana tirumanjanam are performed. Later, the lord is adorned with diamond kavacha on the second day. He is adorned with pearl-studded kavacha and taken out in procession. On the third day Sri Malayappaswami is decorated with golden kavacha after tirumanjanam.

Padmavati parinayam

This festival is celebrated in May. The specially arranged Kalyana Mandapam in the Narayanagiri gardens is the venue of the celestial wedding of Lord Srinivasa and Goddess Padmavathi. Pomp and gaiety mark this three - day celebration performed in the evening. In this colorful ceremony conducted on Navami, Dasami and Ekadasi in the month of Vaisakha, Sri Malayappaswami, the festival deity of

Lord Venkateswara, arrives in style on Gaja, Asva and Garuda Vahanas while Sridevi and Bhudevi arrive on separate palanquins. Every day, after the wedding in the Kalayana Mandapam, 'Koluvu' is held. A number of cultural programmes like Harikatha, dance and music take place. Later the Lord along with Sridevi and Bhudevi return to the temple. Thus, the three-day long grand wedding ceremony comes to a close. Devotees who purchase tickets for the wedding ceremony performed each day can take part in this annual sevas.

Pushpa Pallaki

This seva is performed on Anivara Asthanam and is celebrated on that day usually in the month of July every year. After the usual rituals associated with the Anivara Asthanam, held on the first day of summer solstice (Dakshinayanapunyakalam) at the end of any month, Sri Malayappaswami along with Sridevi and Bhudevi, is taken out in procession on a palanquin bedecked with flowers.

Pavithrotsavam

The object of this festival is expiating of the sins of omission and commission arising in the daily worship and other religious rites performed in the temple. It is, therefore, a purificatory ceremony. The annual pavitrotsavam of Lord Venkateswara is held at Tirumala for three days from the Dasami of the Suklapaksha in the month of sravanam (August).

Pushpa Yagam

This ceremony is performed in the month of (kartika) after annual Brahmotsavam on the occasion of Sravanam. Ankurarpanam is done prior to the Pushpayagam. On this day in the morning, after the daily pujas, Sri Malayappa Swami along with Sridevi and Bhudevi is seated. After offering Tirumanjanam to the utsava murtis worship is done to them with a large variey of flowers. Procession takes place in the evening.

Koil Alwar Thirumanjanam

Koil Alwar means 'Holy Shrine'. The main purpose of performing koil Alwar Tirumanjanam is a purification. It is a ceremony that takes place in the temple including sanctum sanctorum. It is performed four times a year - before Ugadi, Anivara Asthanam, the Annual Brahmotsavam and Vaikunta Eakadasi (on Tuesday only).

After the first bell, the smaller idols and other articles including the akhanda dipams are shifted to the antechamber. The Garbhagriha is then cleaned and a ground paste of kumkum, camphor and sandalwood is applied on the walls and later its walls are wiped clean after a while with water. The waterproof covering is removed and laghu Tirumanjanam is given to the main deity and Bhoga Srinivasa. Food is then offered to the lord during the second bell.

Brahmotsavam of Lord Venkateswara

The brahmotsavam of Lord Venkateswara, the presiding deity of the Seven Hills, is the most splendid and spectacular of all the festivals in Tirumala, though every day is a festival day in Tirumala. This is a nine-day festival. It has its own grandeur and uniqueness. The colorful processions of Lord Venkateswara on all these nine days on various (vehicles), and the throngs of the devotees without any reference to religion, or caste and creed, substantiate the age-old belief that "if there be heaven on earth, it is this, it is this".

Brahmotsavam commences on the day of the ankurarpana, and is followed by the Dwajarohanam the next day. Most important among the utsavams is the Garudaseva (Garudoutsavam) on the fifth day of the Brahmotsavam with the Lord being carried by the garuda without His consort

Endowment Schemes

TTD has initiated several schemes to cater to the demands of the increasing influx of pilgrims to Tirumala, to support the economically backward, and improve the environment in and around Tirumala. It has established a number of trusts like

- Sri Venkateswara Pranadana Trust

- Sri Venkateswara Nitya Laddu Danam Scheme
- Sri Venkateswara Nitya Anna Danam Scheme
- Sri Padmavathi Ammavari Nitya Anna Prasadam Scheme
- Sri Venkateswara Vidyadana Trust Scheme
- Sri Venkateswara Vanabhivruddhi Scheme
- BIRRD Scheme
- Sri Balaji Arogyavaraprasadini Scheme
- Cottage Donation Scheme
- Sri Venkateswara Gosamrakshana Trust
- **Sri Venkateswara Balamandir Trust Scheme**
- Sri Venkateswara Heritage Preservation Trust
- Sri Venkateswara Information Technology Seva Trust
- Sreenivasam Complex Donation Scheme

The above discussion gives a clear picture of the Lord Venkateswara temple, historical development of the T.T.D. administration from the earliest times unto the period of the British rule, history of the management of the T.T.D. Social Activities, Educational Activities, Religious Activities of the temple, facilities and services provided by TTD to devotees.

REFERENCES

1. S.G.S. Bhagavan, Finances of the TTD Educational Institutions, unpublished thesis submitted to S.V.University, Tirupati, 1995 Pg. No.38, 39.

2. T.T.D. Administration Report 1998-99 Pg. No. 2.

3. P.Sitapathi, "Art and Sculpture in Sri Venkateswara Swamy temple", T.T.D Tirupati, 1986, Pg. 24.

4. J. Subramanyam, "Personnel Management in T.T.D." unpublished thesis submitted to S.V.University, Tirupati, 1987 Pg. 36, 37.

5. T.T.D. Administration Report 1998-99 Pg. No. 2, 3.

6. Veeraraghavachary, T.K.T, "History of Tirupati", T.T.D. Vol.1, 1953, Pg.10.

7. K.P. Venkatarathnam Achari, Tirumala Tirupati – A Study in Religion and Society, unpublished thesis submitted to S.V.University, Tirupati, 1992 Pg. No.60.

8. The word "Vengadam" shows Tirumala is considered the holiest among Vishnu Kshetrams in India,

9. P.Sitapathi, Sri Venkateswara, the Lord of the Seven Hills Tirupati: Bharatiya Vidya Bhavan, 1977, Pg. No. 86.

10. T.T.D. Administration Report 1998-99 Pg. No. 1.

11. P. Krishnamurthy, Rayalaseemaloni Mukhya Devalayalu (in Telugu) Tirupati. 1982, Pg.37.

12. Ibid, Ins No. 12 to 42.

13. V.Kameswara Rao, Temples in and around Tirupati, 1986 g.5.

14. The Educational Administration in TTD – A Study. Unpublished thesis submitted to S.V.University, Tirupati, 1995 Pg. No.62 by Vivekananda Reddy.

15. B.S.L. Hanumantha Rao and Basaveswara Rao, "India History and Culture", Vol. III, Guntur: 1983, Pg.69.

16. T. Krishnaswamy, History of Tirumala Tirupati, TTD publications 1980, Pg. 138.

17. T.T.D. Administration Report 1998-99 Pg. No.1.

18. It is an organization founded by Sri Swami Hatheeramji a Great saint who came from northern India to Tirumala with a large number of disciples.

19. T.T.D. Administration Report 1998-99 Pg. No. 1.

20. Rama Swamy Aiyer C., op cit., Pg. No. 24

21. T.T.D. Administration Report 1998-99 Pg. No. 1,2.

22. T.T.D. Administration Report 1998-99 Pg. No. 5.

23. Endowments Act No. 30 of 1987, Section 107 and Subsection (i)

24. Endowments Act No. 30 of 1987, Section 108 and Subsection (i)

Chapter - IV

MEASUREMENT OF ORGANIZATIONAL CLIMATE

This chapter is divided into three sections. Section A presents the socio demographic variables of the select employees of Tirumala Tirupati Devasthanams under study area. Section B is devoted to a study and analysis of the various dimensions of organizational climate of employees. Section C tries to identify the variations in perception on organizational climate among personal variables of employees.

SECTION - A

An attempt is made in the following pages to present the socio demographic variables of the select employees of Tirumala Tirupati Devasthanams.

4. 1. Designation of the Respondents

The designation of the respondents is portrayed in table 4.1. The sample for the study consists of 36 professionals, 109 administrative staff, and 215 sub staff. On the whole, 59.7 per cent of the respondents are the sub staff and the remaining 30.3 per cent are the administrative staff. 10 per cent are the professionals and their responses to the structured questionnaire are the basis for the overall analysis of the study.

Table 4.1
Designation of the Sample Respondents

(N=360)

Designation	Number of Respondents	Per cent
Professionals	36	10.0
Administrative Staff	109	30.3
Sub Staff	215	59.7
Total	**360**	**100.0**

Source: Field Survey

4. 2. Sex-wise Distribution

Table 4.2 shows Sex-wise Distribution of the sample respondents. It is observed from the table that, 68.3 per cent of the respondents in the sample are males and the rest are females. Further, the female employees, category-wise, are also found to be limited in number.

Based on chi-square test, it can be inferred that there is a significant difference between professionals, administrative staff, and sub staff with respect to sex.

Table 4.2
Sex-wise Distribution of the Sample Respondents

(N=360)

Sex	Category of staff				Chi-Square
	Professional staff	Administrative Staff	Sub Staff	Grand Total (N= 360)	
Male	32 (88.9)	95 (87.2)	119 (55.3)	246 (68.3)	$\chi 2 = 41.627**$
Female	4 (11.1)	14 (12.8)	96 (44.7)	114 (31.7)	
Total	36 (100.0)	109 (100.0)	215 (100.0)	360 (100.0)	DF= 2

Source: Field Survey

Note : Figures in parentheses are percentages to respective column totals.

** Significant at 1 per cent level

4.3. Age- wise Distribution

The age wise distribution of the sample respondents is shown in table 4.3. It is evident from the table that a majority of the respondents (37.2 per cent) belong to the age group of 36-40, as well as 32.8 per cent respondents belong to the age group of 41-45, 18.9 per cent respondents belong to the age group of 31-35 and a few respondents belonging to the age group of 46 and above are 5.8 per cent and below 30 age group are 5.3 per cent.

The chi-square value is significant at 1 per cent level. Thus, it can be inferred that there is a significant difference between professionals, administrative staff, and sub staff with respect to age.

Table 4.3
Age- wise Distribution of the Sample Respondents

(N=360)

| Age | Category of staff | | | | Chi-Square |
	Professional staff	Administrative Staff	Sub Staff	Total	
Below 30	0 (0)	12 (11)	7 (3.3)	19 (5.3)	
31-35	14 (38.9)	41 (37.6)	13 (6)	68 (18.9)	
36 - 40	12 (33.3)	29 (26.6)	93 (43.3)	134 (37.2)	$\chi 2$ = 78.049**
41 - 45	10 (27.8)	19 (17.4)	89 (41.4)	118 (32.8)	DF= 8
46 & Above	0 (0)	8 (7.3)	13 (6)	21 (5.8)	
Total	36 (100)	109 (100)	215 (100)	360 (100)	

Source: Field Survey

Note : Figures in parentheses are percentages to respective column totals.

** The Chi-square statistic is significant at 0.01 level.

4.4 Marital Status - wise Distribution

Table 4.4 shows the marital status of the respondents. It can be noted from the table that 86.7 per cent of the respondents, on the whole, are married while 13.3 per cent are unmarried. The professional-respondents (22.2 per cent) are unmarried as well as administrative staff respondents (17.4 per cent) and sub staff respondents are 9.8 per cent respectively. The chi-square value is significant at 5 per cent level. It can be inferred that there is a significant difference between professionals, administrative staff, and sub staff with respect to marital status.

Table 4.4
Marital Status - wise Distribution of the Sample Respondents

(N=360)

| Marital Status | Category of staff | | | | Chi-Square |
	Professional staff	Administrative Staff	Sub Staff	Total	
Married	28 (77.8)	90 (82.6)	194 (90.2)	312 (86.7)	
Unmarried	8 (22.2)	19 (17. 4)	21 (9.8)	48 (13.3)	$\chi 2$ = 6.411*
Total	36 (100)	109 (100)	215 (100)	360 (100)	DF= 2

Source: Field Survey

Note: Figures in parentheses are percentages to respective column totals.

* The Chi-square statistic is significant at 0.05 level.

4.5. Social Status - wise Distribution

Table 4.5 presents social status wise distribution of sample respondents. It is noted from the table that, 36.4 per cent of respondents belong to other caste community, 32.8 per cent are from backward classes, 19.2 per cent belong to scheduled caste and 11.7 per cent of respondents are from scheduled tribe community. Category- wise sample respondents also indicate a similar trend. The chi-square value is significant at 5 per cent level. It can be inferred that there is a significant difference between professionals, administrative staff, and sub staff with respect to social status.

Table 4.5
Social Status - wise Distribution of the Sample Respondents

(N=360)

Social Status	Category of staff			Grand Total (N= 360)	Chi-Square
	Professional staff	Administrative Staff	Sub Staff		
OC	13 (36.1)	31 (28.4)	87 (40.5)	131 (36.4)	
BC	10 (27.8)	41 (37.6)	67 (31.2)	118 (32.8)	$\chi2 = 13.095$ *
SC	12 (33.3)	19 (17.4)	38 (17.7)	69 (19.2)	DF = 6
ST	1 (2.8)	18 (16.5)	23 (10.7)	42 (11.7)	
Total	**36 (100)**	**109 (100)**	**215 (100)**	**360 (100)**	

Source: Field Survey
Note : Figures in parentheses are percentages to respective column totals.
* Significant at 5 per cent level

4.6. Family Size - wise Distribution

Size of the family is one of the important factors that determines both income and savings of the people. In this regard a question is put to the respondents regarding the size of the families. All such details are presented in table 4.6. It is evident that most of respondents are in the family size of four (39.2 per cent). About 23.6 per cent of the respondents have 3 members in their families, 18.1 per cent have 5 members in their families and 14.7 per cent have above 5 members. From this one can deduce that the respondents in the present study prefer to have smaller families. The chi-square value is significant at 1 per cent level. It can be inferred that there is a significant

94

difference between professionals, administrative staff, and sub staff with respect to family size.

Table 4.6
Family Size - wise Distribution of the Sample Respondents

Family Size	Category of staff				Chi-Square
	Professional staff	Administrative Staff	Sub Staff	Grand Total (N360)	
Two	2 (5.6)	0 (0)	14 (6.5)	16 (4.4)	
Three	10 (27.8)	32 (29.4)	43 (20)	85 (23.6)	
Four	6 (16.7)	39 (35.8)	96 (44.7)	141 (39.2)	$\chi 2 = 22.485**$
Five	8 (22.2)	21 (19 3)	36 (16.7)	65 (18.1)	DF = 8
Above 5	10 (27.8)	17 (15.6)	26 (12.1)	53 (14.7)	
Total	36 (100)	109 (100)	215 (100)	360 (100)	

Source: Field Survey
Note: Figures in parentheses are percentages to respective column totals.
       ** The Chi-square statistic is significant at 0.01 level.

4.7. Family BackGround

The classification of respondents by family background is presented in table 4.7. It shows that 36.7 per cent of the   employees selected for the study have an agriculture background. Similarly, 24.4 per cent respondents are from service families, 24.2 per cent of the employees are from others and 14.7 per cent of employees have come from business families.

Table 4.7
Family Back Ground - wise Distribution of the Sample Respondents

(N=360)

Family Back Ground	Category of staff				Chi-Square
	Professional staff	Administrative Staff	Sub Staff	Grand Total (N360)	
Agriculture	13 (36.1)	38 (34.9)	81 (37.7)	132 (36.7)	
Business	4 (11.1)	19 (17.4)	30 (14)	53 (14.7)	$\chi 2 = 3.129$ NS
Service	10 (27.8)	30 (27.5)	48 (22.3)	88 (24.4)	
Others	9 (25.0)	22 (20.2)	56 (26)	87 (24.2)	DF = 6
Total	**36 (100)**	**109 (100)**	**215 (100)**	**360 (100)**	

Source: Field Survey

Note: Figures in parentheses are percentages to respective column totals.
The Chi-square statistic not significant at 0.05 level

4.8. Type of Family

It can be observed from table 4.8 that majority of respondents, 53.6 per cent, belong to nuclear families. This is because now-a-days people prefer to live independently rather than in a joint family set up and the remaining 46.4 per cent are from joint families. In this regard there is not much difference among professionals, administrative staff and sub staff respondents.

Table 4.8
Type of Family - wise Distribution of the Sample Respondents

(N=360)

Type of Family	Category of staff				Chi- Square
	Professional staff	Administrative Staff	Sub Staff	Grand Total (N360)	
Joint Family	15 (41.7)	50 (45.9)	102 (47.4)	167 (46.4)	$\chi 2 = 0.430$ NS
Nuclear Family	21 (58.3)	59 (54.1)	113 (52.6)	193 (53.6)	DF = 2
Total	**36 (100)**	**109 (100)**	**215 (100)**	**360 (100)**	

Source: Field Survey

Note: Figures in parentheses are percentages to respective column totals.
The Chi-square statistic not significant at 0.05 level

4.9. Total Earning Members in the Family

The total earning members in the families of respondents are displayed in table 4.9. It is found from the table that category-wise, 16 professional respondents, 69 administrative staff respondents' and138 Sub Staff respondents have only one earning member. This may be because of the fact that, in India, the tradition is that men prefer to do job while women comparatively are reluctant. However, of late, the current trend is gradually changing. It is also noticed from the table that families with two earning members constitute 26.4 per cent, families with three earners constitute 10.6 per cent and about 1.1 per cent of the families have four or more earning members.

The chi-square value is significant at 1 per cent level. It can be inferred that there is a significant difference between professionals, administrative staff, and sub staff with respect to total earning members in the family.

Table 4.9
Total Earning Members in the Family-wise Distribution of the Sample Respondents

(N=360)

Total Earning Members in the Family	Category of staff				Chi-Square
	Professional staff	Administrative Staff	Sub Staff	Grand Total (N360)	
One	16 (44.4)	69 (63.3)	138 (64.2)	223 (61.9)	$\chi2 = 19.300**$ DF = 6
Two	9 (25)	29 (26.6)	57 (26.5)	95 (26.4)	
Three	9 (25)	9 (8.3)	20 (9.3)	38 (10.6)	
Four	2 (5.6)	2 (1.8)	0 (0)	4 (1.1)	
Total	**36 (100)**	**109 (100)**	**215 (100)**	**360 (100)**	

Source: Field Survey
Note : Figures in parentheses are percentages to respective column totals.
**The Chi-square statistic is significant at 0.01 level

4.10. Total Family Annual Income

The details of total family annual income among the households are presented in table 4.10. It is clear from the table that 52 respondents (14.4 per cent) earn less than Rs. 1.5 lakhs, 184 respondents (15.1 per cent) have Rs. 1.5-2.0 lakhs, 83 respondents earn between Rs. 2.0-2.5 lakhs and 41 respondents earn Rs. 2.5 lakhs and above. The figures also reveal that category-wise staff are not similar, i.e., professional respondents are 58.3 per cent earning 2.50 lakhs and above, administrative staff respondents are 65.1 per cent earning 1.50- 2.0 lakhs and sub staff respondents are 50.7 per cent earning 1.50-2.0 lakhs.

The chi-square value is significant at 1 per cent level. It can be inferred that there is a significant difference between professionals, administrative staff, and sub staff with respect to total family annual income.

Table 4.10
Total Family Annual Income - wise Distribution of the Sample Respondents
(N=360)

Total Family Annual Income	Category of staff				Chi-Square
	Professional staff	Administrative Staff	Sub Staff	Grand Total(N360)	
Below Rs. 50,000	1 (2.8)	10 (9.2)	41 (19.1)	52 (14.4)	
Rs. 50,001 - Rs. 2,00,000	4 (11.1)	71 (65.1)	109 (50.7)	184 (51.1)	$\chi2 = 103.375**$
Rs. 2,00,001 - Rs. 2,50,000	10 (27.8)	20 (18.3)	53 (24.7)	83 (23.1)	DF = 6
Rs. 2,50,001 Above	21 (58.3)	8 (7.3)	12 (5.6)	41 (11.4)	
Total	**36 (100)**	**109 (100)**	**215 (100)**	**360 (100)**	

Source: Field Survey
Note : Figures in parentheses are percentages to respective column totals.
**The Chi-square statistic is significant at 0.01 level.

4.11. Educational Qualifications

The details of educational qualifications are shown in table 4.11. Most of the respondents studied tenth standard. About 23 respondents are in the education qualification intermediate, 88 respondents are in the education qualification graduate, 60 respondents are in the education qualification post graduate, and few respondents i.e. 6.9 per cent have professional's degrees.

The chi-square value is significant at 1 per cent level. It can be inferred that there is a significant difference between professionals, administrative staff, and sub staff with respect to educational qualification.

Table 4.11
Educational Qualifications - wise Distribution of the Sample Respondents
(N=360)

Educational Qualifications	Category of staff				Chi-Square
	Professional staff	Administrative Staff	Sub Staff	Grand Total (N360)	
Below 10th Standard	0 (0)	0 (0)	164 (76.3)	164 (45.6)	
Intermediate	0 (0)	17 (15.6)	6 (2.8)	23 (6.4)	
Graduate	5 (13.9)	53 (48.6)	30 (14)	88 (24.4)	$\chi 2 = 311.002$**
Post Graduate	13 (36.1)	32 (29.4)	15 (7)	60 (16.7)	DF = 8
Professionals degree	18 (50)	7 (6.4)	0 (0)	25 (6.9)	
Total	**36 (100)**	**109 (100)**	**215 (100)**	**360 (100)**	

Source: Field Survey

Note : Figures in parentheses are percentages to respective column totals.
      **The Chi-square statistic is significant at 0.01 level

4.12. Technical Qualifications

Technical qualification details of the respondents are presented in table 4.12. It can be found from the table that 277 respondents (77 per cent) have no technical qualification, very few employees i.e., 9 per cent, have typing, 8 per cent have PGDCA, 4 per cent DCA, and 1.4 per cent have B.Tech qualification.

The chi-square value is significant at 1 per cent level. It can be inferred that there is a significant difference between professionals, administrative staff, and sub staff with regard to technical qualification.

Table 4.12
Distribution of Sample Respondents According to their Technical Qualification
(N=360)

Technical Qualifications	Category of staff				Chi-Square
	Professional staff	Administrative Staff	Sub Staff	Grand Total (N360)	
No Technical Qualification	11 (30.6)	51 (46.8)	215 (100)	277 (76.9)	
Typing	5 (13.9)	29 (26.6)	0 (0)	34 (9.4)	
DCA	1 (2.8)	13 (11.9)	0 (0)	14 (3.9)	$\chi^2 = 227.957**$
PGDCA	14 (38.9)	16 (14.7)	0 (0)	30 (8.3)	DF = 8
B.Tech	5 (13.9)	0 (0)	0 (0)	5 (1.4)	
Total	36 (100)	109 (100)	215 (100)	360 (100)	

Source: Field Survey

Note : Figures in parentheses are percentages to respective column totals.
**The Chi-square statistic is significant at 0.01 level

4.13. Monthly Salary

Monthly salary particulars of the selected respondents are shown in table 4.13. The table shows that 40 per cent respondents are in the monthly salary range of 10,001-15,000 followed by 33.6 per cent respondents in the monthly salary range of Rs. 15,001-20,000, 18.1 per cent respondents are in the monthly salary range of below 10,000 and 8 per cent of respondents in the monthly salary of above 20.001.

The chi-square value is significant at 1 per cent level. It can be inferred that there is a significant difference between professionals, administrative staff, and sub staff with respect to monthly salary.

Table 4.13
Classification of Sample Respondents According to Monthly Salary

(N=360)

| Monthly Salary | Category of staff | | | | Chi-Square |
	Professional staff	Administrative Staff	Sub Staff	Grand Total (N360)	
Below Rs 10,000	0 (0)	37 (33.9)	28 (13)	65 (18.1)	
Rs.10001 -Rs.15000	7 (19.4)	38 (34.9)	99 (46)	144 (40)	$\chi2 = 192.008**$
Rs.15001-Rs.20,000	6 (16.7)	27 (24.8)	88 (40.9)	121 (33.6)	DF = 6
20,001 & Above	23 (63.9)	7 (6.4)	0 (0)	30 (8.3)	
Total	**36 (100)**	**109 (100)**	**215 (100)**	**360 (100)**	

Source: Field Survey
Note : Figures in parentheses are percentages to respective column totals.
**The Chi-square statistic is significant at 0.01 level

4.14. No. of Years of Service

Table 4.14 presents the details of no. of years of service of the respondents. It is noted that 23.9 per cent of respondents are in 16-20 and 20 years and above service category in TTD; it reveals that the respondents who have put in 11-15 years of service accounted for 27.8 per cent, while below 5 years respondents are 13.3 per cent and 6-10 years of respondents are 11.1 per cent.

The chi-square value is significant at 1 per cent level. It can be inferred that there is a significant difference between professionals, administrative staff, and sub staff with respect to number of years of service.

Table 4.14
No. of Years Service - wise Distribution of the Sample Respondents
(N=360)

No. of Years of service in TTD	Category of staff				Chi-Square
	Professional staff	Administrative Staff	Sub Staff	Grand Total (N360)	
Below 5	5 (13.9)	31 (28.4)	12 (5.6)	48 (13.3)	
6 -10	12 (33.3)	18 (16.5)	10 (4.7)	40 (11.1)	
11- 15	7 (19.4)	28 (25.7)	65 (30.2)	100 (27.8)	$\chi2 = 76.683**$
16-20	4 (11.1)	22 (20.2)	60 (27.9)	86 (23.9)	DF = 8
20 & Above	8 (22.2)	10 (9.2)	68 (31.6)	86 (23.9)	
Total	36 (100)	109 (100)	215 (100)	360 (100)	

Source: Field Survey
Note : Figures in parentheses are percentages to respective column totals.
**The Chi-square statistic is significant at 0.01 level

4.15. No. of Promotions

The details of number of promotions received so far by the respondents are presented in table 4.15. It shows that on the whole, most of the sample employees (73.3 per cent) received no promotion. Further, the table reveals that 19 per cent of respondents have received promotions once, and 6.9 per cent of respondents received promotion twice. The chi-square value is significant at 1 per cent level. From this it can be inferred that there is a significant difference between professionals, administrative staff, and sub staff with respect to number of promotions received.

Table 4.15

No. of Promotions - wise Distribution of the Sample Respondents

(N=360)

No. of Promotions received sofar in TTD	Category of staff				Chi-Square
	Professional staff	Administrative Staff	Sub Staff	Grand Total (N360)	
Nil	12 (33.3)	53 (48.6)	199 (92.6)	264 (73.3)	$\chi2 = 111.977**$ DF = 6
Once	18 (50)	42 (38.5)	10 (4.7)	70 (19.4)	
Twice	5 (13.9)	14 (12.8)	6 (92.8)	25 (6.9)	
Three Times	1 (2.8)	0 (0)	0 (0)	1 (3)	
Total	36 (100)	109 (100)	215 (100)	360 (100)	

Source: Field Survey

Note : Figures in parentheses are percentages to respective column totals.

      ** The Chi-square statistic is significant at 0.01 level.

4.16. No. of Awards and Rewards

Table 4.16 exhibits the details of awards and rewards either in the form of money or in the form of letter of appreciation by the respondents. It is surprised to notice that the majority, 98 per cent of the respondents, did not receive any kind of awards and rewards in their career. Very few respondents have received monetary awards and rewards (1.1 per cent). Only 6 per cent of respondents have received non-monetary awards and rewards.

The chi-square value is significant at 5 per cent level. It can be inferred that there is a significant difference between professionals, administrative staff, and sub staff with respect to number of awards and rewards.

Table 4.16

No. of Awards & Rewards - wise Distribution of the Sample Respondents

(N=360)

No. of Awards & Rewards	Category of staff				Chi-Square
	Professional staff	Administrative Staff	Sub Sub Staff	Grand Total (N360)	
Not Received	35 (97.2)	104 (95.4)	215 (100)	354 (98.3)	
Monetary	1 (2.8)	3 (2.8)	0 (0)	4 (1.1)	$\chi2 = 10.696*$
Non-Monetary	0 (0)	2 (1.8)	0 (0)	2 (6)	DF = 4
Total	**36 (100)**	**109 (100)**	**215 (100)**	**360 (100)**	

Source: Field Survey

Note : Figures in parentheses are percentages to respective column totals.

* The Chi-square statistic is significant at 0.05 level.

4.17. No. Of Employee Training Programmes

Details of training programmes attended by the select employees are seen in table 4.17. It is witnessed that except 145 respondents, 40 per cent all the respondents have attended the training programmes. Further, it is observed that among 22.2 per cent of respondents professionals 3, administrative staff 16, and sub staff 61 respondents attended training programmes once, and those who attended training programmes 4 or more times professionals are 13.9 per cent, administrative staff are 22 per cent and sub staff respondents, 20 per cent, respectively.

The chi-square value is significant at 5 per cent level. It can be inferred that there is a significant difference between professionals, administrative staff, and sub staff with respect to number of training programmes attended.

Table 4.17
No. of Employee Training Programme - wise Distribution of the
Sample Respondents

(N=360)

No. Of Employee Training Programmes Attended	Category of staff				Chi-Square
	Professional staff	Administrative Staff	Sub Staff	Grand Total (N360)	
Not Attended	13 (36.1)	32 (29.4)	100 (46.5)	145 (40.3)	
One Time	3 (8.3)	16 (14.7)	61 (28.4)	80 (22.2)	
Two Times	9 (25)	15 (13.8)	0 (0)	24 (6.7)	$\chi 2$ = 73.053**
Three Times	6 (16.7)	22 (20.2)	11 (5.1)	39 (10.8)	DF = 8
Four Times & Above	5 (13.9)	24 (22)	43 (20)	72 (20)	
Total	36 (100)	109 (100)	215 (100)	360 (100)	

Source: Field Survey
Note : Figures in parentheses are percentages to respective column totals.
** The Chi-square statistic is significant at 0.01 level.

SECTION - B

An attempt in the following pages are made to study and analyse dimensions of organizational climate as perceived by the selected employees. The organizational climate is examined with the help of 19 dimensions containing 79 statements. The 19 dimensions include:

Managerial Structure and policies; Recognition and appreciation; Participative Management; Supervision; Conflict avoidance; warmth; Social Values; Training and advancement; Grievance Handling; Individual Autonomy; Individual Responsibility; Performance Standards; Mutual Trust; Awards and rewards system; Work Relation; Decision-Making; Welfare facilities; Communication; and unions.

4.18. Managerial structure and policies

These are concerned with interest and evaluations of ideas from subordinates by the management; constraints felt by the employees; quick and accurate decision-making; degree to which the leader is open, supportive and considerate towards his followers/subordinates.

Table 4.18shows the perceptions of respondents on the Managerial structure and policies. The respondents moderately accept that 'The policies and goals of the T.T.D are clearly understood' (3.49). 'In TTD the formal authority takes decisions' (3.39). 'The job in TTD is clearly defined and structured logically' (3.39) and 'The TTD recruits people after objective assessment of the merits of each case' (3.33). 'Information relating to job or policy is communicated to employee through established channels' (2.96) and 'Service rules and policies are consistently followed in TTD while dealing with the employee's personal matters' (3.08).

Therefore, it can be said that management can influence organizational climate by changing policies, rules and procedure .This may take time, but the change is long lasting if the employees see the change in policies as favourable to them.

Table 4.18
Perceptions on Managerial structure and policies

(N=360)

S.No	Statements	Mean	Standard Deviation
1	The policies and goals of the T.T.D are clearly understood	3.49	0.929
2	Service rules and policies are consistently followed in TTD while dealing with the employees personal matters	3.08	0.994
3	Information relating to job or policy is communicated to employee through established channels	2.96	1.086
4	The TTD recruits people after objective assessment of the merits of each case	3.33	1.007
5	In TTD the formal authority takes decisions	3.39	0.904
6	The job in TTD is clearly defined and structured logically	3.39	1.131

4.19. Recognition and Appreciation

Recognition and appreciation of sincere and hard working employees and of those contributing to the productivity and efficiency of the organization is crucial for the success of the organization.

According to table 4.19, respondents well agreed with the statements 'I feel that I am a valuable member of a team working in TTD' (3.74), 'In TTD, the management always recognizes good work' (3.58) and 'There is recognition for merit, talent and qualifications in TTD' (3.41) shows that the working team is on the higher side. There is a weak agreement (2.85) with the view 'Suggestions given by me for improvement are well appreciated recognized by superior' and (3.10) 'The work of mine is done by colleagues' better manner he/she will get proper recognition'. So, it can be said that the Recognition and Appreciation is fairly common in TTD organization.

Table 4.19
Perceptions on Recognition and Appreciation

(N=360)

S.No	Statements	Mean	Standard Deviation
1	I feel that I am a valuable member of a team working in TTD	3.74	1.006
2	In TTD, the management always recognizes good work	3.58	1.081
3	There is recognition for merit, talent and qualifications in TTD	3.41	0.895
4	The work of mine is shared by colleagues' they will get proper recognition	3.10	1.040
5	Suggestions given for me for improvement are well appreciated and recognized by superiors	2.85	1.213

4.20. Participative Management

Involvement of employees in solving day-to-day problems; competency and effective performance of various committees; recognition given to workers' representatives in meetings; negotiation in decision-making.

Perception on sharing of power and decision-making are presented in table 4.20.The respondents have indicated some agreement with the view that management is participative. The view- 'before taking any important decision, the management of TTD always consults the employees' (2.89) is less acceptable and the statements 'The management gives due respect and power to the workers representatives in meetings' (3.3 1) is moderately agreeable. The view' the representatives of various committees in TTD are capable and competent (3.13)' is less agreeable. The TTD organization gives due respect to workers' representatives, but there is less participative management in TTD organization.

Table 4.20
Perceptions on Participative Management

(N=360)

S.No	Statements	Mean	Standard Deviation
1	The management gives due respect and power to the workers representatives in meetings	3.31	0.858
2	Before taking any important decision, the management always in TTD always consults the	2.89	0.862
3	The representatives of various committees in TTD are capable and competent	3.13	0.790

4.21. Supervision

Supervision practices contribute significantly to climate and atmosphere. If supervisors focus on helping their subordinates to improve personal skills and chances of advancement, a climate that is characterized by the extension motive may result. If supervisors are more concerned with maintaining good relations with their subordinates, a climate characterized by the affiliation motive may result.

Table 4.21 shows the views of respondents. They are close to agreement with the statements, 'The main purpose of supervision is to ensure achievement of targets' (3.63) follows, 'Superiors in our organization expect subordinates to do the job strictly according to rules' (3.53),'Supervision in our organization helps to maintain good relations with subordinate' (3.47) and 'My superiors give help and support'

(3.40). There is moderate agreement with the views- 'Superiors in our organization usually check mistakes and punish subordinates' (3.19) and 'My superior listens to what I have to say' (3.02). From this, it can be concluded that supervision is perceived as fair in TTD organization.

Table 4.21
Perceptions on Supervision

(N=360)

S.No	Statements	Mean	Standard Deviation
1	Supervision in our organization ensure to maintain good relations with subordinate	3.47	0.886
2	Superiors in our organization usually check mistakes and punish subordinates	3.19	0.871
3	My superiors give help and support for my employees	3.40	1.037
4	My superior listens to what I have to say	3.02	1.165
5	Superiors in our organization expect subordinates to do the job strictly according to rules	3.53	0.870
6	The main purpose of supervision is to ensure achievement of targets	3.63	0.776

4.22. Conflict Avoidance

Life is a never ending process of one conflict after the other, thus conflicts are enevitable in life. Conflicts occur at various levels within the individuals, between the individuals in a group and between the groups.

Table 4.22 presents the perception on conflict avoidance. The respondents have shown agreement with the statements that indicate- "Conflicts are usually avoided and people prefer friendly atmosphere in TTD' (3.68), and 'Experts are consulted and their advice is sought in resolving conflicts' (3.45), the perception shows that conflict avoidance system is well organised in TTD organization.

109

Table 4.22
Perceptions on Conflict Avoidance

(N=360)

S.No	Statements	Mean	Standard Deviation
1	Conflicts are usually avoided and people prefer friendly atmosphere in TTD	3.68	0.903
2	Experts are consulted and their advice are sought in resolving conflicts	3.45	0.906

4.23. Warmth

Relaxed and easy-going working climate; lot of warmth in the relationship between management and employees; a friendly atmosphere prevails among the employees.

From table 4.23, it is obvious that respondents perceive this dimension positively. They agree that, 'A Friendly atmosphere prevails among the employees in TTD' (3.71) they also perceive 'There is a lot of warmth in the relationship between management and employees in TTD' (3.39) and 'In TTD there is a relaxed and easy going working climate' (3.25). In view of this, it can be said that the warmth is reasonably good.

Table 4.23
Perceptions on Warmth

(N=360)

S.No	Statements	Mean	Standard Deviation
1	In TTD there is a relaxed and easy going working climate	3.25	0.969
2	There is a lot of warmth in the relationship between management and employees in TTD	3.39	0.860
3	A Friendly atmosphere prevails among the employees in TTD	3.71	0.854

4.24. Social Values

Management should encourage social group activities by the employees. This will help to develop greater group cohesiveness which can be used by the management for building favourable organizational climate.

According to table 4.24 respondents have agreed well with the statements." I am proud to be a member of TTD' (4.08)", they have also agreed that 'I have high satisfaction that I am rendering social service to the society through TTD' (4.01), 'The management of TTD encourages us to take part in social service and cultural programmes' (3.91) and also 'TTD organization gives special attention to fulfill the social needs of the employees, in order to increase their social values' (3.49). The findings indicate that employees are proud to be members in this organization and Social Values in TTD organization are protected very well.

Table 4.24
Perceptions on Social Values

(N=360)

S.No	Statements	Mean	Standard Deviation
1	TTD organization gives special attention to fulfill the social needs of the employees, in order to increase	3.49	1.094
2	I am proud to be a member of TTD	4.08	0.817
3	The management of TTD encourages us to take part in social service and cultural programmes	3.91	0.991
4	I have high satisfaction that I am rendering social service to the society through TTD	4.01	0.826

4.25. Training and Advancement

Table 4.25 shows that the respondent's views - 'adequate training programmes and facilities' (3.71), as well as 'I have had sufficient job related training' (3.48), 'TTD plans on regular basis for ensuring its employees the career development' (3.33) and 'opportunities for their career advancement' (3.29), are available in TTD organization. Therefore, it can be said that the dimension- Training and Advancement- is perceived as fair in TTD organization. But change in training and advancement; there should be ample scope for growth of each person in an organization and organization must strive for overall development of staff. New CEO brings such changes after joining the TTD organisation

Table 4.25
Perceptions on Training and Advancement

(N=360)

S.No	Statements	Mean	Standard Deviation
1	TTD provides adequate training programmes and facilities to its employees	3.71	0.959
2	Employees in TTD have many opportunities for their career advancement	3.29	0.865
3	TTD plans on regular basis for ensuring its employees the career development	3.33	0.931
4	I have had sufficient job related training	3.48	0.899

4.26. Grievance Handling

The three statements – as per the grievance handling in TTD, it is perceived by the employees that 'The TTD is always ready to handle the grievances and complaints of the employees' (3.14) 'The grievance handling and settlement system existing in the TTD is effective' (3.03) and I am satisfied with the present system of grievance handling procedure in TTD (3.04) as shown in table 4.26 is moderately acceptable to the respondents. Therefore, it can be stated that grievance handling is above average and requires further improvement.

Table 4.26
Perceptions on Grievance Handling

(N=360)

S.No	Statements	Mean	Standard Deviation
1	The TTD always ready to handle the grievances and complaints of the employees	3.14	1.085
2	The grievance handling and settlement system existing in the TTD is effective	3.03	1.141
3	I am satisfied with the present system of grievance handling procedure in TTD	3.04	1.083

4.27. Individual Autonomy

It is the degree of freedom from accountability to others. By this we mean employees are free to manage themselves and have considerable decision making power.

Table 4.27 presents the perception on individual autonomy. The respondents have shown themselves to be undecided with the statements that indicate 'Employees are free to set their own performance goals' (3.09) and 'work gives me opportunity of freedom and independence' (3.00). This is indicative of Individual Autonomy the TTD employees have at work place.

Table 4.27
Perceptions on Individual Autonomy

(N=360)

S.No	Statements	Mean	Standard Deviation
1	Employees are free to set their own performance goals in TTD	3.09	1.070
2	My work gives me opportunity of freedom and independence	3.00	1.121

4.28. Individual Responsibility

Table 4.28 shows the perception on individual responsibility. The respondents have agreed well with the statements – 'I always feel responsible at work' (3.76) and 'If at times things do not go well, I do take responsibility' (3.74). From this, it can be concluded that individual responsibility is perceived well by the respondents.

Table 4.28
Perceptions on Individual Responsibility

(N=360)

S.No	Statements	Mean	Standard Deviation
1	I always feel responsible at work	3.76	0.945
2	If at times things do not go well, I do take responsibility	3.74	0.827

4.29. Performance Standards

Table 4.29 the respondents have shown moderate agreement with the statements – 'In TTD importance is given for high quality of work' (3.30) as well as 'The problems that are relating to work are solved quickly' (3.30) It follows, 'The goals that are set by the TTD are communicated to all the members to achieve them' (3.26) 'In TTD we set very high Standards for performance' (3.25) 'In TTD without any delay with regard to work' (3.23) and 'There are rules and regulations for handling any kind of problem, which may arise in making most of the decisions'(2.97). From this, it can be understood that reasonable standards are maintained for better performance and it needs further improvement.

Table 4.29
Perceptions on Performance Standards

(N=360)

S.No	Statements	Mean	Standard Deviation
1	In TTD we set very high Standards for performance	3.25	1.085
2	There are rules and regulations for handling any kind of problem, which may arise in making most of the decisions	2.97	1.198
3	The goals that are set by the TTD are communicated to all the members to achieve them	3.26	0.929
4	The problems that are relating to work are solved quickly	3.30	0.996
5	In TTD without any delay with regard to work	3.23	0.854
6	In TTD importance is given for high quality of work	3.30	0.927

4.30. Mutual Trust

Table 4.30 presents the perception on mutual trust. The respondents are well agreed with the statements that indicate- 'Employees in this organization really trust each other very much' (3.52), 'There is high trust between superiors and subordinates in the TTD organization' (3.38) as well as 'Specialists and experts are highly trusted in TTD' (3.38)'and 'Those who can achieve good results in the TTD organization are highly trusted' (3.19). From this, it can be understood that there is a reasonable level of mutual trust.

114

Table 4.30
Perceptions on Mutual Trust

(N=360)

S.No	Statements	Mean	Standard Deviation
1	Those who can achieve good results in the TTD organization are highly trusted	3.19	0.927
2	There is high trust between superiors and subordinates in the TTD organization	3.38	0.940
3	Employees in this organization really trust each other very much	3.52	0.807
4	Specialists and experts are highly trusted in TTD	3.38	0.924

4.31. Awards and rewards system

Table 4.31 portrays statements relating to Awards and rewards system. The respondents are neutral to the statements- 'Employees who keeping up the tradition in this organization are duly recognized and rewarded' (3.22), it follows 'The management of TTD recognizes the efficiency of one's own work and accordingly employees are awarded' (3.12), 'Team work in the TTD organization is encouraged and rewarded' (3.08), 'Any thing goes wrong with the employees, such employees are seriously reprimanded or punished' (3.05) and 'Excellence in performance and getting tasks accomplished are highly rewarded in the TTD organization(2.85).

It may be concluded that change reward system as culture is learned, it can also be unlearned. Revised systems establish and reinforce specific cultural behaviours and therefore, a change in culture can be initiated and supported by changes incorporated in the reward system.

Table 4.31
Perceptions on Awards and rewards system

(N=360)

S. No	Statements	Mean	Standard Deviation
1	Excellence in performance and getting tasks accomplished are highly rewarded in the TTD	2.85	0.972
2	Employees who keep up the tradition in this organization are duly recognized and rewarded	3.22	0.944
3	Team work in the TTD organization is encouraged and rewarded	3.08	0.839
4	If anything goes wrong with the employees such employees are seriously reprimanded or punished	3.05	0.890
5	The management of TTD recognizes the efficiency of one's own work and accordingly employees are	3.12	0.960

4.32. Work Relation

The perceptions of respondents on Work Relation are shown in table 4.32. It reveals that 'the relations among the colleagues in our organization are healthy and friendly' (3.77) 'Employees in TTD are very much concerned to help each other spontaneously when ever need arises' (3.61) and 'The working relations between superiors and subordinates in TTD are so cordial' (3.45).). From this, it can be concluded that Work Relations in TTD are perceived well by the respondents.

Table 4.32
Perceptions on Work Relation

(N=360)

S.No	Statements	Mean	Standard Deviation
1	The working relations between superiors and subordinates in TTD are so cordial	3.45	0.888
2	The relations among the colleagues in our organization more healthy and friendly	3.77	0.756
3	Employees in TTD are very much concern to help each other spontaneously when ever need arises	3.61	0.876

4.33. Decision Making

Table 4.33 shows that the respondents disagree with the statements that indicate –'decisions are made in consultation with the unions in TTD' (2.79), mainly the experts are involved in the decision making process' (2.76)', and how often are you involved in decision making' (2.14). The findings indicate that employees are not involved in decision-making process. The employees should be involved in goal setting and taking decisions influencing their lot. They will feel committed to the organization and exhibit an attitude of co-operation.

Table 4.33
Perceptions on Decision Making

(N=360)

S.No	Statements	Mean	Standard Deviation
1	Decisions are made in consultation with the unions in TTD	2.79	0.752
2	Mainly the experts are involved in the decision making process	2.76	0.725
3	How often are you involved in decision making	2.14	1.168

4.34. Welfare Facilities

Management must provide for employees welfare measures like canteens, credit facilities, sports clubs, education facilities for their children, etc. Management's concern for employees' welfare will increase the goodwill of the management in the eyes of the employees.

The perceptions of respondents on welfare facilities are shown in table 4.34. The respondents have agreed well with the statements, 'Medical facilities/ medical reimbursement provided by the employer are adequate' (3.84). It is followed by 'The Management of TTD provides adequate and qualitative educational services to the children of employees' (3.63), 'TTD administration provides housing accommodation with water facilities at reasonable cost' (3.48), 'I am convenient with the transport facilities from home to the work place' (3.47), 'TTD provides attractive retirement benefits to its employees' (3.58) and ' The welfare facilities provided by TTD are far

117

better than the welfare facilities provided by Govt'(3.44). From this, it can be concluded that welfare facilities are perceived very well by respondents in TTD organization.

Table 4.34
Perceptions on Welfare Facilities

(N=360)

S.No	Statements	Mean	Standard Deviation
1	Medical facilities/ medical reimbursement provided by the employer are adequate	3.84	0.930
2	The Management of TTD provides adequate and qualitative educational services to the	3.63	0.863
3	TTD administration provides housing accommodation with water facilities at reasonable	3.48	1.047
4	I am convenient with the transport facilities from home to the work place	3.47	1.081
5	TTD provides attractive retirement benefits to its employees	3.58	0.847
6	The welfare facilities provided by TTD are far better than the welfare facilities provided by Govt.	3.44	0.988

4.35. Communication

There should be two- way communication between the management and the employees as it exercises a profound influence on organizational climate. The employees should be kept informed about the organization policies and programmes through conferences, bulletins and informal discussions with the employees. They should be allowed to ask questions and satisfy themselves about their doubts.

The perceptions of respondents on communication are shown in table 4.35.There is moderate agreements with the statements- 'One way communication that is from top to bottom is in vogue in TTD' (3.30). It is followed by 'Upward communication is accurate in our organization' (3.18) as well as 'There is good communication across all sections in' (3.11) 'Relevant information is available to all those who need and can use such information' (3.14) 'Employees taking initiative in

118

communicating concern for others' (3.03) and 'Communication between subordinates and superiors is always open' (3.13).

From this, it can be concluded that the respondents perceive communication as positive and improved communication; there should be two-way communication in the organization so that the employees know what is going on and react to it. The management can modify its decisions on the basis of employee's reaction.

Table 4.35
Perceptions on Communication

(N=360)

S.No	Statements	Mean	Standard Deviation
1	One way communication that is from top to bottom is in vogue in TTD	3.30	0.886
2	Upward communication is accurate in our organization	3.18	0.870
3	There is good communication across all sections in TTD	3.11	1.005
4	Relevant information is available to all those who need and can use such information	3.14	0.908
5	Employees are taking initiative in communicating concern for others	3.03	1.092
6	Communication between subordinates and superiors is always open	3.13	0.934

4.36. Unions

From table 4.36 it is obvious that respondents perceive this dimension with moderate agreement expressing views such as -'TTD is not opposing the formation and functioning of the unions' (3.32) as well as 'Trade union leadership is acquired on democratic lines in our organization' (3.18). It followed by views like 'Issues for collective bargaining are determined with the consultation of union members', (3.17) 'Unions in my organization are effective in solving their problems of the employees' (3.11), 'There is no inter-union rivalry in this organization'(3.06) and 'Union-management relations are cordial'(3.01). As such, it can be said that the dimension union is perceived as positive in TTD organization.

Table 4.36
Perceptions on Unions

(N=360)

S.No	Statements	Mean	Standard Deviation
1	TTD is not opposing the formation and functioning of the unions	3.32	0.757
2	Trade union leadership is acquired on democratic lines in our organization	3.18	0.841
3	There is no inter-union rivalry in this organization	3.06	0.954
4	Issues for collective bargaining are determined with the consultation of union members	3.17	0.886
5	Unions in my organization are effective in solving their problems of the employees	3.11	0.735
6	Union-management relations are cordial	3.01	0.964

4.37. Rating of organizational climate dimension

What are the perceptions of respondents on OC dimension? Table 4.37 shows the perceptions of the respondents on OC dimension. The entire dimension is positively viewed by the respondents but on decision making dimension it is less agreeable. The mean scores are in the range of 2.56 to 3.87 on a 5-point scale indicating every dimension of organization's climate is moderately agreeable to the respondents.

Table 4.37
Perceptions of Respondents on OC dimensions

(N=360)

S.No	OC Dimensions	Mean	Standard Deviation
1	Managerial Structure and policies	3.27	1.01
2	Recognition and appreciation	3.34	1.05
3	Participative Management	3.11	0.84
4	Supervision	3.37	0.93
5	Conflict avoidance	3.57	0.90
6	Warmth	3.45	0.89
7	Social Values	3.87	0.93
8	Training and advancement	3.45	0.91
9	Grievance Handling	3.07	1.10
10	Individual Autonomy	3.05	1.10
11	Individual Responsibility	3.75	0.89
12	Performance Standards	3.22	1.00
13	Mutual Trust	3.37	0.90
14	Awards and rewards system	3.06	0.92
15	Work relation	3.61	0.84
16	Decision Making	2.56	0.88
17	Welfare Facilities	3.57	0.96
18	Communication	3.15	0.95
19	Unions	3.14	0.86

SECTION - C

ORGANISATIONAL CLIMATE AND PERSONAL VARIABLES

With reference to each of the personal variables i.e, gender, age, income, education and experience, dimension wise analysis of perception of respondents' employees on organizational climate is presented in Table 4.38 to 4.44. To find out if there are significant differences of organizational climate across each variable, the respondents are analyzed using z-test. Under each group, means and standard deviations are calculated for each dimension of OC. F-value for large sample means was performed for each organizational climate dimension.

4.38 Perception Across Gender

Table 4.38 furnishes the results of z-test on means for each dimension across gender. Therefore, it can be concluded that gender has no influence on the perceptions of the organizational climate. Therefore, the hypothesis formulated that there is no significant difference between gender and organizational climate is accepted.

Table 4.38
Perceptions of Respondents on OC dimensions – Across Gender

(N=360)

S. No	OC Dimensions	Male (N= 246)		Females (N=114)		Z-values
		Mean	SD	Mean	SD	
1	Managerial Structure and policies	3.329	0.844	3.158	0.505	2.383*
2	Recognition and appreciation	3.348	0.962	3.309	0.491	0.512
3	Participative Management	3.114	0.722	3.096	0.546	0.253
4	Supervision	3.396	0.709	3.323	0.364	1.283
5	Conflict avoidance	3.602	0.926	3.478	0.546	1.582
6	Warmth	5.142	1.104	5.241	0.621	-1.084
7	Social Values	3.909	0.864	3.798	0.457	1.580
8	Training and advancement	3.424	0.757	3.515	0.519	-1.337
9	Grievance Handling	2.915	1.026	3.406	0.593	-5.731*
10	Individual Autonomy	2.984	1.001	3.180	0.701	-2.141**
11	Individual Responsibility	3.652	0.956	3.952	0.352	-4.319*
12	Performance Standards	3.281	0.792	3.085	0.472	2.927*
13	Mutual Trust	3.370	0.817	3.364	0.574	0.079
14	Awards and rewards system	2.933	0.752	3.344	0.409	-6.686*
15	Work relation	3.560	0.825	3.722	0.530	-2.250**
16	Decision Making	2.782	0.674	2.102	0.619	9.411*
17	Welfare Facilities	3.518	0.789	3.692	0.356	-2.870**
18	Communication	3.066	0.783	3.328	0.378	-4.278*
19	Union	3.083	0.621	3.262	0.473	-3.001*
20	Overall Climate	3.331	0.577	3.376	0.289	-0.947

Note: * *Significant at 1 per cent level
* Significant at 5 per cent level, NS = Not Significant

122

4.39 Perceptions Across Age

Table 4.39 furnishes the results of F-test for each dimension across the three age groups viz., lower age (< 30 years), middle age (30 years to 35 years) and higher age (35 years and above). Under each age group, means and standard deviations are calculated for each dimension of organizational climate and F-values are performed to detect statistically significant differences across age group. Statistically significant difference across age group has been found for 6 out of 19 dimensions of organizational climate. These are: Managerial Structure and policies, supervision, social Values, awards and rewards system, work relation, and welfare Facilities.

Therefore, lower age group (< 30 years) influences the perceptions of the organizational climate. Therefore, the hypothesis formulated that there is significant difference between age and organizational climate is rejected.

Table 4.39
Perceptions of Respondents on OC dimensions – Across Age

(N=360)

S. No	OC Dimensions	Lower (N= 87)		Middle (N=134)		Higher (N=139)		F-Value
		Mean	SD	Mean	SD	Mean	SD	
1	Managerial Structure and policies	3.523	0.685	3.264	0.720	3.129	0.799	7.516**
2	Recognition and appreciation	3.393	0.791	3.324	0.850	3.311	0.867	0.276NS
3	Participative Management	3.103	0.690	3.192	0.630	3.031	0.691	1.965NS
4	Supervision	3.513	0.545	3.409	0.565	3.249	0.695	5.327 *
5	Conflict avoidance	3.661	0.693	3.604	0.781	3.460	0.933	1.861NS
6	Warmth	5.230	0.952	5.239	0.765	5.076	1.158	1.143NS
7	Social Values	4.043	0.736	3.957	0.572	3.687	0.890	7.406**
8	Training and advancement	3.451	0.640	3.549	0.643	3.362	0.757	2.517NS
9	Grievance Handling	3.226	0.923	3.090	0.984	2.954	0.895	2.300NS
10	Individual Autonomy	3.190	0.931	2.981	0.891	3.018	0.937	1.459NS
11	Individual Responsibility	3.753	0.828	3.776	0.767	3.716	0.883	0.184NS
12	Performance Standards	3.284	0.707	3.235	0.643	3.163	0.775	0.822NS
13	Mutual Trust	3.391	0.743	3.424	0.709	3.300	0.787	0.978 NS
14	Awards and rewards system	3.271	0.632	3.170	0.624	2.830	0.721	14.522**
15	Work relation	3.579	0.744	3.614	0.621	3.628	0.857	0.120NS
16	Decision Making	2.893	0.652	2.585	0.767	2.345	0.657	16.475**
17	Welfare Facilities	3.552	0.671	3.706	0.536	3.458	0.799	4.609*
18	Communication	3.216	0.654	3.154	0.605	3.101	0.787	0.756NS
19	Union	3.146	0.466	3.195	0.528	3.083	0.690	1.278NS
	Overall Climate	3.455	0.455	3.392	0.393	3.230	0.599	6.467**

Note: * * Significant at 1 per cent level
* Significant at 5 per cent level, NS= Not significant

4.40 Perceptions Across   Monthly Salary

To find out if there is significant difference in the perception on organizational climate across the income levels of respondents, the perceptions are tabulated in Table 4. 40 across different income groups. Income groups are classified into lower income (up to Rs. 10,000), middle income (Rs. 10,001 to Rs. 20,000) and higher income (more than Rs. 20,000) groups. Under each income group, means and standard deviations were calculated for each dimension of organizational climate. F-test is done for each organizational climate dimension across income to know the statistically significant differences. Statistically significant differences are found in respect of 11 out of 19 items. They are:

Managerial Structure and policies; Recognition and appreciation; Supervision; Conflict avoidance; Social Values; Individual Responsibility; Performance Standards; Mutual Trust; Awards and rewards system; decision-making; and welfare facilities;

Therefore, it can be said that monthly salary of higher level income (more than Rs. 20,000) groups has greater   influence on the perception on organizational climate. So, the hypothesis formulated that there is significant difference between monthly salary and organizational climate is rejected

Table 4.40
Perceptions of Respondents on OC dimensions – Across Monthly Salary
(N=360)

S. No	OC Dimensions	Lower (N= 144)		Middle (N=121)		Higher (N=95)		F-Value
		Mean	SD	Mean	SD	Mean	SD	
1	Managerial Structure and policies	3.193	0.684	3.136	0.818	3.574	0.705	10.824**
2	Recognition and appreciation	3.296	0.794	3.212	0.881	3.554	0.825	4.770**
3	Participative Management	3.086	0.632	3.201	0.688	3.025	0.698	1.993NS
4	Supervision	3.323	0.550	3.310	0.703	3.528	0.592	4.120*
5	Conflict avoidance	3.479	0.795	3.475	0.880	3.800	0.759	5.471*
6	Warmth	5.233	0.834	5.054	1.167	5.237	0.908	1.375NS
7	Social Values	3.870	0.656	3.709	0.910	4.089	0.644	6.894**
8	Training and advancement	3.462	0.638	3.353	0.756	3.566	0.671	2.556NS
9	Grievance Handling	3.130	0.889	3.019	0.995	3.046	0.945	0.498NS
10	Individual Autonomy	3.038	0.861	3.000	0.970	3.116	0.947	0.428NS
11	Individual Responsibility	3.743	0.753	3.620	0.885	3.916	0.834	3.465**
12	Performance Standards	3.110	0.626	3.222	0.802	3.381	0.686	4.223*
13	Mutual Trust	3.269	0.705	3.207	0.750	3.724	0.695	16.070**
14	Awards and rewards system	3.201	0.603	2.823	0.718	3.160	0.701	11.833**
15	Work relation	3.549	0.707	3.601	0.813	3.719	0.715	1.515NS
16	Decision Making	2.535	0.796	2.397	0.688	2.832	0.591	10.205**
17	Welfare Facilities	3.575	0.632	3.464	0.764	3.709	0.644	3.420*
18	Communication	3.144	0.628	3.132	0.774	3.177	0.680	0.118NS
19	Union	3.112	0.574	3.116	0.638	3.212	0.522	0.996NS
20	Overall Climate	3.337	0.454	3.236	0.580	3.496	0.432	7.378**

Note: ** Significant at 1 per cent level
* Significant at 5 per cent level, NS = Not Significant

4.41 Perceptions Across Education

On the basis of educational level, respondents were divided into three groups viz., highly educated (post graduate and above), moderately educated (graduates) and low education (intermediate and below). The details are presented in Table 4.41. F-test is done for each organizational climate dimension across education to know the statistically significant differences. Statistically significant differences are found in respect of 13 out of 19 items. They are:

Managerial Structure and policies; Recognition and appreciation; Supervision; Conflict avoidance; Social Values; Training and advancement; Grievance Handling; Individual Autonomy; Performance Standards; Mutual Trust; Awards and rewards system; decision-making; and welfare facilities;

The results indicate that higher education has shown greater influence on the perception on organizational climate dimension. So, the hypothesis formulated that there exists significant difference between education and organizational climate is rejected.

Table 4.41
Perceptions of Respondents on OC dimensions – Across Education

(N= 360)

S. No	OC Dimensions	Intermediate & Others (N=206)		Graduate (N=75)		PG & Above (N=79)		F-Value
		Mean	SD	Mean	SD	Mean	SD	
1	Managerial Structure and policies	3.100	0.746	3.400	0.801	3.610	0.598	15.366**
2	Recognition and appreciation	3.267	0.799	3.219	1.049	3.625	0.652	6.279**
3	Participative Management	3.116	0.680	3.147	0.756	3.051	0.555	0.428NS
4	Supervision	3.306	0.626	3.404	0.720	3.517	0.473	3.464*
5	Conflict avoidance	3.434	0.833	3.793	0.886	3.677	0.680	6.351**
6	Warmth	5.124	1.009	5.313	0.996	5.171	0.869	1.035NS
7	Social Values	3.677	0.729	4.017	0.745	4.250	0.688	19.740**
8	Training and advancement	3.370	0.710	3.577	0.759	3.551	0.533	3.516*
9	Grievance Handling	3.055	0.884	2.898	1.175	3.274	0.789	3.197*
10	Individual Autonomy	2.971	0.842	2.913	1.128	3.367	0.831	6.466**
11	Individual Responsibility	3.672	0.818	3.853	0.853	3.842	0.811	1.994NS
12	Performance Standards	3.089	0.739	3.396	0.745	3.390	0.510	8.369**
13	Mutual Trust	3.268	0.755	3.570	0.764	3.437	0.670	5.014*
14	Awards and rewards system	2.975	0.702	3.152	0.817	3.210	0.460	4.182*
15	Work relation	3.568	0.735	3.738	0.715	3.603	0.803	1.428NS
16	Decision Making	2.330	0.693	2.933	0.662	2.835	0.645	29.859**
17	Welfare Facilities	3.493	0.660	3.640	0.692	3.719	0.728	3.613*
18	Communication	3.156	0.690	3.073	0.753	3.200	0.637	0.676NS
19	Union	3.140	0.622	3.182	0.626	3.099	0.421	0.388NS
20	Overall Climate	3.247	0.516	3.427	0.542	3.522	0.356	10.279**

Note: * *Significant at 1 per cent level
* Significant at 5 per cent level NS = Not Significant

4.42 Perceptions Across Experience

Table 4.42 examines the influence of experience on the perceptions of respondents. Based on length of service, three groups are formed: low (up to 10 years), medium (10 years to 15 years) and high (more than 16 years) groups were classified. F-test is done for each organizational climate dimension across experience to know the statistically significant differences. Statistically significant differences are found in respect of 12 out of 19 items. They are:

Managerial Structure and policies; Recognition and appreciation; Conflict avoidance; warmth; Social Values; Grievance Handling; Individual Responsibility; Awards and rewards system; work relation; decision-making; welfare facilities; and communication.

The results indicate that low (up to 10 years) service group has shown greater influence on the perception on organizational climate dimension. Therefore, the hypothesis formulated that there is significant difference between service and organizational climate is rejected.

Table 4.42
Perceptions of Respondents on OC dimensions – Across Service

N= (360)

S. No	OC Dimensions	Lower (N=88)		Middle (N=100)		Higher (N=172)		F-Value
		Mean	SD	Mean	SD	Mean	SD	
1	Managerial Structure and policies	3.563	0.896	3.190	0.939	3.176	1.062	8.801**
2	Recognition and appreciation	3.471	0.983	3.104	0.998	3.401	1.066	5.586**
3	Participative Management	3.000	0.872	3.183	0.798	3.120	0.817	1.809NS
4	Supervision	3.489	0.787	3.338	0.888	3.334	0.997	2.043NS
5	Conflict avoidance	3.648	0.714	3.680	0.785	3.451	1.035	3.096*
6	Warmth	3.424	0.857	3.583	0.776	3.384	0.967	3.088*
7	Social Values	4.026	0.851	3.920	0.873	3.769	0.973	3.626¹
8	Training and advancement	3.543	0.928	3.433	0.913	3.419	0.898	0.996NS
9	Grievance Handling	3.296	1.041	3.173	1.185	2.895	1.049	6.301**
10	Individual Autonomy	3.137	1.084	3.045	1.134	3.000	1.076	0.638NS
11	Individual Responsibility	3.847	0.891	3.940	0.602	3.584	0.987	6.926**
12	Performance Standards	3.212	1.035	3.233	0.914	3.214	1.024	0.028NS
13	Mutual Trust	3.435	0.984	3.343	0.811	3.349	0.891	0.463NS
14	Awards and rewards system	3.348	0.937	3.306	0.782	2.777	0.897	33.731**
15	Work relation	3.572	0.900	3.793	0.670	3.525	0.876	4.314**
16	Decision Making	2.955	0.940	2.390	0.851	2.471	0.804	18.544**
17	Welfare Facilities	3.636	0.998	3.708	0.734	3.462	1.030	4.644**
18	Communication	3.246	0.883	3.335	0.870	2.991	0.988	9.437**
19	Union	3.222	0.799	3.188	0.766	3.070	0.914	2.470NS
20	Overall Climate	3.487	0.477	3.375	0.307	3.255	0.586	6.618**

Note: ** Significant at 1 per cent level
* Significant at 5 per cent level, NS = Not Significant

4.43 Perceptions Across Designation

Table 4.43 shows perception of respondents on organizational climate dimensions-across designations.

Table 4.43
Perceptions of Respondents on OC dimensions – Across Designation

N= (360)

S. No	OC Dimensions	Professionals (n=36)		Administrative Staff (n=109)		Sub-Staff (215)		F-Value
		Mean	SD	Mean	SD	Mean	SD	
1	Managerial Structure and policies	3.806	0.462	3.544	0.571	3.049	0.791	29.333*
2	Recognition and appreciation	3.661	0.494	3.594	0.713	3.15	0.896	14.067*
3	Participative Management	3.028	0.543	3.073	0.7	3.139	0.675	0.638NS
4	Supervision	3.593	0.469	3.619	0.49	3.211	0.652	20.051*
5	Conflict avoidance	3.847	0.619	3.862	0.531	3.363	0.916	17.005*
6	Warmth	5.389	0.776	5.523	0.682	4.96	1.074	13.878*
7	Social Values	4.312	0.501	4.154	0.587	3.658	0.798	24.954*
8	Training and advancement	3.535	0.604	3.585	0.673	3.372	0.705	3.764**
9	Grievance Handling	3.241	0.795	3.346	0.953	2.902	0.92	9.117*
10	Individual Autonomy	3.5	0.765	3.358	0.895	2.812	0.884	19.419*
11	Individual Responsibility	4.167	0.707	4.023	0.554	3.537	0.892	19.476*
12	Performance Standards	3.574	0.455	3.339	0.67	3.098	0.739	9.571*
13	Mutual Trust	3.625	0.622	3.631	0.661	3.192	0.759	16.063*
14	Awards and rewards system	3.4	0.422	3.305	0.693	2.885	0.668	20.114*
15	Work relation	3.639	0.845	3.804	0.607	3.509	0.777	5.847*
16	Decision Making	3.074	0.672	2.749	0.694	2.389	0.694	20.543*
17	Welfare Facilities	3.884	0.578	3.745	0.572	3.434	0.722	12.215*
18	Communication	3.315	0.623	3.396	0.642	2.995	0.687	14.263*
19	Union	3.32	0.46	3.197	0.482	3.081	0.639	3.386**
20	Overall Climate	3.616	0.273	3.554	0.391	3.194	0.528	27.883*

Note: * Significant at 1 per cent level
** Significant at 5 per cent level, NS = Not Significant

F-test is done for each organizational climate dimension across designation to know the statistically significant differences. Statistically significant differences are found in respect of 18 out of 19 items. The results indicate that professionals group has shown greater influence on the perception on organizational climate dimensions. So, the hypothesis formulated that there exists significant difference between designation and organizational climate is rejected

4.44 Correlation analysis

Table 4.44
Correlation between OC and Demographic Variables

N= (360)

S. No	OC Dimensions	Gender	Age	Monthly Salary	Education	Service
1	Managerial Structure and policies	-0.105*	-0.197**	0.184**	0.281**	-0.190**
2	Recognition and appreciation	-0.022NS	-0.036NS	0.109*	0.150**	-0.002NS
3	Participative Management	-0.012NS	-0.055NS	-0.24NS	-0.032NS	0.059NS
4	Supervision	-0.054NS	-0.169**	0.122*	0.138*	-0.093NS
5	Conflict avoidance	-0.070NS	-0.098*	0.145**	0.146**	-0.110*
6	Warmth	0.047NS	-0.068NS	-0.009NS	0.035NS	-0.47NS
7	Social Values	-0.068NS	-0.191**	0.096NS	0.314**	-0.140**
8	Training and advancement	0.062NS	-0.065NS	0.047NS	0.122*	-0.068NS
9	Grievance Handling	0.244**	-0.113*	-0.040NS	0.070NS	-0.181**
10	Individual Autonomy	0.099NS	-0.064NS	0.029NS	0.151**	-0.059NS
11	Individual Responsibility	0.169**	-0.021NS	0.070NS	0.094NS	-0.151**
12	Performance Standards	-0.129**	-0.067NS	0.151**	0.193**	-0.001NS
13	Mutual Trust	-0.004NS	-0.054NS	0.222**	0.118*	-0.042NS
14	Awards and rewards system	0.277**	-0.261**	-0.054NS	0.147**	-0.367**
15	Work relation	0.101NS	0.025NS	0.089NS	0.038NS	-0.052NS
16	Decision Making	-0.434**	-0.290**	0.141**	0.327**	-0.236**
17	Welfare Facilities	0.117*	-0.073NS	0.063NS	0.139**	-0.122*
18	Communication	0.176**	-0.065NS	0.017NS	0.013NS	-0.176**
19	Union	0.142**	-0.052NS	0.064NS	-0.019NS	-0.112*
20	Overall Climate	0.042NS	-0.181**	0.107*	0.231**	-0.189**

Note: **Significant at 1 per cent level
    * Significant at 5 per cent level
N.S :   Not significant

131

Correlation between OC and demographic variables is presented in table 4.44.To further examine the validity of the hypothesis, correlations between the personal variables such as age, gender, income, education and experience and perceptions of respondent employees on organizational climate scores are found. Table 4.43 shows a lack of association of the perceptions with age, gender, income, education and experience variables has significant correlation at 0.01level with about 12 of the dimensions and also with overall climate. However, the coefficients are negative and below 0.05 indicating a weak negative relationship.

Chapter - V

MEASUREMENT OF JOB SATISFACTION

The respondents are asked to rate their opinions on five point scale viz., highly satisfied (score-5), satisfied (score-4), undecided (score-3), dissatisfied (score-2), and highly dissatisfied with one score. For the present study, a set of 20 variables, which are related to job are asked on a five point scale and they elicited responses from the TTD employees.

The scoring weight for each item ranged from 1 to 5 and possible scores varied from 20 to 100. The job satisfaction of TTD employees of different categories is discussed in this section. The following procedure is adopted to classify the employees into three job satisfaction levels. First Mean ($\overline{X}$) is calculated, dividing aggregate satisfaction scores by 360 respondents 25158 / 360 = 69.88 points. The value of standard deviation (S.D.) calculated is 12.12 points. When the score value is more or equal to $\overline{X}$ + 1.S.D, it is high satisfaction level. When score value is equal to or less than $\overline{X}$ – 1.S.D. it is low level satisfaction level. When score value is more than $\overline{X}$ -1.S.D. but less than $\overline{X}$ + 1.S.D, it is moderately level of satisfaction.

The following are high, low, moderate levels of satisfaction.

High-Level: (Mean + S.D) = (69.88 + 12.12) =82

Low-Level: (Mean – S.D.) = (69.88 – 12.12) =58

Moderate level: >58 and < 82 Satisfaction Sores

Guided by high, medium, and low satisfaction scores the following the tables are drawn putting the sample respondents in each satisfaction category or into the aforementioned three levels

Association between Personal Aspects of the employees and Job Satisfaction among the employees of TTD

An attempt is made in the following pages to analyse the relationship between personal aspects of the selected employees of Tirumala Tirupati Davasthanams and the level of job satisfaction. Association of personal characteristics like age, sex, marital status, social status, family size, family background, type of family, total earning members in the family, total family annual income, education qualification, technical qualification, monthly salary, no of years service, no of promotions received, no of awards and rewards received, and no of employee training programmes attended with the job satisfaction was found out by using chi- square test of significance.

5. 1. Designation and Level of Job Satisfaction

It is evident from table 5.1 that the majority of respondents (45.45 per cent) are administrative staff and are in high satisfaction category. The respondents who are professionals (10.99 per cent), sub staff (59.22 per cent), and administrative staff (29.79 per cent) are in moderate satisfaction levels, whereas the majority of respondents, (85.29 per cent) who are sub staff, fall in low satisfaction level. The chi-square value is given by 15.603 which is highly significant at 1 per cent level. It reveals that there is significant association between designation and job satisfaction. The null hypothesis formulated for job satisfaction is rejected.

Table 5.1
Designation and Level of Job Satisfaction

(N = 360)

Level of Job Satisfaction	Designation				Chi-Square
	Professionals	Administrative Staff	Sub Staff	Total	
High	5 (11.36)	20 (45.45)	19 (43.18)	44 (100)	$\chi 2 = 15.603**$
Moderate	31 (10.99)	84 (29.79)	167 (59.22)	282 (100)	
Low	0 (0.00)	5 (14.71)	29 (85.29)	34 (100)	DF= 4
Total	**36 (10.00)**	**109 (30.28)**	**215 (59.72)**	**360 (100)**	

Source: Field Survey

Note : Figures in parenthesis are percentages to respective column totals.

    **Significant at 0.01 per cent level.

5. 2. Sex and Level of Job Satisfaction

Table 5.2 presents sex-wise job satisfaction among the selected respondents. It is found that majority of the respondents, 86.36 per cent, 62.41 per cent, and 94.12 per cent of male employees are having high, moderate, and low satisfaction levels respectively when compared to female respondents.

There is a general feeling that there exists an association between sex and job satisfaction. It is proved in the present study. The chi-square value given is 21.627which is highly significant at 1 per cent level. It reveals that there is significant association between sex and job satisfaction. The null hypothesis formulated for job satisfaction is rejected.

Table 5.2
Sex and level of Job Satisfaction

(N = 360)

Level of Job Satisfaction	Sex			Chi-Square
	Male	Female	Total	
High	38 (86.36)	6 (13.64)	44 (100)	$\chi^2 = 21.627**$ DF= 2
Moderate	176 (62.41)	106 (37.59)	282 (100)	
Low	32 (94.12)	2 (5.88)	34 (100)	
Total	**246** (**68.33**)	**114** (**31.67**)	**360** (**100.00**)	

Source   : Field Survey
Note   : Figures in parenthesis are percentages to respective column totals.
             **Significant at 0.01 per cent level.

5. 3. Age and Level of Job Satisfaction

Age is supposed to have some relation to job satisfaction. However, when the data were categorized according to high, medium and low satisfaction groups and five age categories (table 5.3) and tested for association, the chi-square value given is 37.749which is highly significant at 1 per cent level. It reveals that there is significant association between age and job satisfaction. However, 40.91 per cent of respondents in the age group of 36-40 are in high satisfaction level. As well as majority of the respondents (5.67 per cent) are in the age group below 30, 19.15 per cent of respondents are in age group between 31-35, and 32.62 per cent of respondents are in age group between 41 -45. They are having moderate level satisfaction. Majority of the respondents in the age group of 46 and above (26.47 per cent) fall in the low satisfaction category. The null hypothesis formulated for job satisfaction is rejected.

Table 5.3
Age and Level of Job Satisfaction

(N = 360)

Level of Job Satisfaction	Age						Chi-square
	Below 30	31-35	36 - 40	41 - 45	46 & Above	Total (N=360)	
High	2 (4.55)	12 (27.27)	18 (40.91)	11 (25.00)	1 (2.27)	44 (100)	$\chi 2 = 37.749**$
Moderate	16 (5.67)	54 (19.15)	109 (38.65)	92 (32.62)	11 (3.90)	282 (100)	
Low	1 (2.94)	2 (5.88)	7 (20.59)	15 (44.12)	9 (26.47)	34 (100)	DF= 8
Total	19 (5.28)	68 (18.89)	134 (37.22)	118 (32.78)	21 (5.83)	360 (100)	

Source: Field Survey
Note : Figures in parenthesis are percentages to respective column totals.
   **Significant at 0.01 per cent level.

5.4. Marital Status and Level of Job Satisfaction

It is clear from table 5.4 that majority of the respondents (79.55 per cent, 86.52per cent, and 97.06per cent) are married employees. Their satisfaction levels are high, medium, and low respectively. Some studies indicated that married employees have some added responsibilities as compared to unmarried employees. As a result, married employees have better adjustment to their work situation and, hence, higher job satisfaction than unmarried employees. These indicate that marital status has no impact on level of satisfaction. Chi-square values computed also are found to be not significant in marital status. Thus, it can be concluded that there is no significant relationship between marital status and job satisfaction. The null hypothesis is accepted.

137

Table 5.4
Marital Status and Level of Job Satisfaction

(N = 360)

Level of Job Satisfaction	Marital Status			Chi-Square
	Married	Unmarried	Total	
High	35 (79.55)	9 (20.45)	44 (100)	χ^2= 5.113NS
Moderate	244 (86.52)	38 (13.48)	282 (100)	
Low	33 (97.06)	1 (2.94)	34 (100)	DF= 2
Total	**312 (86.67)**	**48 (13.33)**	**360 (100)**	

Source: Field Survey
Note : Figures in parenthesis are percentages to respective column totals.
N.S : Not Significant

5.5. Social Status and Level of Job Satisfaction

Table 5.5 reveals the details of social status and job satisfaction. It is noticed from the table that the majority of (50 per cent) respondents in OC are in high job satisfaction whereas, 25.00 per cent of respondents in BC, 11.36 per cent of respondents are in SC, and 13.64 per cent of respondents are in ST category are high satisfaction levels. The chi-square value is given by 12.995which is significant at 5 per cent level. It reveals that there is significant association between social status and job satisfaction. The null hypothesis formulated job satisfaction is rejected.

Table 5.5

Social Status and Level of Job Satisfaction

(N = 360)

Level of Job Satisfaction	Social Status					Chi-square
	OC	BC	SC	ST	Total	
High	22 (50.00)	11 (25.00)	5 (11.36)	6 (13.64)	44 (100)	χ^2 12.995*
Moderate	91 (32.27)	99 (35.11)	61 (21.63)	31 (10.99)	282 (100)	
Low	18 (52.94)	8 (23.53)	3 (8.82)	5 (14.71)	34 (100)	DF= 6
Total	131 (36.39)	118 (32.78)	69 (19.17)	42 (11.67)	360 (100)	

Source: Field Survey

Note : Figures in parenthesis are percentages to respective column totals
*Significant at 0.05 levels

5.6. Family Size and Level of Job Satisfaction

Generating employees having smaller families (having less number of dependents) will be relatively more satisfied than those having larger families. Table 5.6 reveals that the relationship between family size and level of job satisfaction. 29.55 per cent of respondents belonging family size 3 and 4 are in high satisfaction groups whereas, 42.20 per cent of respondents belonging family size four fall in moderate satisfaction level and 29.41 per cent of respondents belonging family size three are in low satisfaction level. Chi- square value is not significant. Thus is, it can be understood that there is no association between family size and job satisfaction. So, the null hypothesis accepted.

Table 5.6
Family Size and Level of Job Satisfaction

(N = 360)

Level of Job Satisfaction	Family Size						Chi-square
	Two	Three	Four	Five	Above 5	Total	
High	0 (0.00)	13 (29.55)	13 (29.55)	7 (15.91)	11 (25.00)	44 (100)	χ2 = 14.650NS
Moderate	16 (5.67)	62 (21.99)	119 (42.20)	50 (17.73)	35 (12.41)	282 (100)	
Low	0 (0.00)	10 (29.41)	9 (26.47)	8 (23.53)	7 (20.59)	34 (100)	DF= 8
Total	**16 (4.44)**	**85 (23.61)**	**141 (39.17)**	**65 (18.06)**	**53 (14.72)**	**360 (100)**	

Source: Field Survey
Note : Figures in parenthesis are percentages to respective column totals
N.S : Not significant at 5 per cent level.

5.7. Family Background and Level of Job Satisfaction

Family background of the employees and their level of job satisfaction details are presented in Table 5.7. The table shows that the majority (36.36 per cent) of respondents with agriculture as family background have reported high satisfaction, whereas some respondents (35.82 per cent and 44.12 per cent) with an agriculture family background belong to moderate and low satisfaction groups respectively. 17.38 per cent of respondents with a business family background belong to moderate satisfaction groups, whereas, 9.09 per cent fall in the high satisfaction range 25 per cent of respondents with service as family back ground are having high satisfaction, whereas, 35.29 per cent of respondents have low satisfaction. With regard to other family back ground, 29.55 per cent have perceived high satisfaction, whereas 20.59 per cent have low satisfaction. The chi-square value is not significant. There is no relationship between family background and job satisfaction. So, the null hypothesis is accepted.

140

Table 5.7
Family Background and level of Job Satisfaction

(N = 360)

Level of Job Satisfaction	Family Back Ground					Chi-Square
	Agriculture	Business	Service	Others	Total	
High	16 (36.36)	4 (9.09)	11 (25.00)	13 (29.55)	44 (100)	χ2 = 10.467NS
Moderate	101 (35.82)	49 (17.38)	65 (23.05)	67 (23.76)	282 (100)	
Low	15 (44.12)	0 (0.0)	12 (35.29)	7 (20.59)	34 (100)	DF= 6
Total	**132** (**36.67**)	**53** (**14.72**)	**88** (**24.44**)	**87** (**24.17**)	**360** (**100**)	

Source: Field Survey

Note : Figures in parenthesis are percentages to respective column totals

N.S : Not significant at 5 per cent level

5.8. Type of Family and Level of Job Satisfaction

Type of family (joint/ nuclear) may be an important factor of job satisfaction. Table 5.8 shows distribution of respondents according to type of family and level of job satisfaction. It can be noticed from the table 5.8 that the majority of respondents 54.55 per cent belong to joint family type. About 45.45 per cent of respondents belonging to nuclear type of family are in high satisfaction group.58.16 per cent of respondents belonging to nuclear family type fall in moderate satisfaction group, and 73.53 per cent of respondents belonging to joint family type fall in the low satisfaction group. The chi-square value is given by 13.590which is highly significant at 1 per cent level. It reveals that there is significant association between type of family and job satisfaction. The null hypothesis formulated for job satisfaction is rejected.

Table 5.8
Type of Family and Level of Job Satisfaction

(N = 360)

Level of Job Satisfaction	Type of Family			Chi-Square
	Joint Family	Nuclear Family	Total	
High	24 (54.55)	20 (45.45)	44 (100)	
Moderate	118 (41.84)	164 (58.16)	282 (100)	$\chi^2 = 13.590$**
Low	25 (73.53)	9 (26.47)	34 (100)	DF= 2
Total	**167 (46.39)**	**193 (53.61)**	**360 (100)**	

Source: Field Survey
Note : Figures in parenthesis are percentages to respective column totals
** Significant at 0.01 per cent level

5.9. Total Earning Members in the Family and Level of Job satisfaction

Table 5.9 shows low employees belong to high 59.09 per cent, moderate 59.22 per cent and low 88.24 per cent job satisfaction groups and belong to families with earning members 29.08 per cent of the respondents perceived moderate satisfaction group, 20.45 per cent of respondents have high job satisfaction, whereas 11.76 per cent of the respondents have low job satisfaction groups is two earning members in the family. 18.18 per cent of respondents have high job satisfaction group is three earning member in the family, whereas 2.27 per cent of respondents have high satisfaction groups is four and above earning members in the family. Therefore, it can be confirmed that there exists no relationship between total earning members in the family and job satisfaction. Chi-square value is not significant. Hence, the null hypothesis is accepted.

Table 5.9
Total Earning Members in the Family and Level of Job satisfaction

(N = 360)

Level of Job Satisfaction	Total Earning Members					Chi-Square
	One	Two	Three	Four and above	Total	
High	26 (59.09)	9 (20.45)	8 (18.18)	1 (2.27)	44 (100)	
Moderate	167 (59.22)	82 (29.08)	30 (10.64)	3 (1.06)	282 (100)	χ2 = 10.467
Low	30 (88.24)	4 (11.76)	0 (0.0)	0 (0.0)	34 (100)	NS
Total	223 (61.94)	95 (26.39)	38 (10.56)	4 (1.11)	360 (100)	DF= 6

Source: Field Survey
Note : Figures in parenthesis are percentages to respective column totals
NS : Not significant at 5 per cent level

5.10. Total Family Annual Income and Level of Job Satisfaction

Income is also a significant factor of job satisfaction. If the employees feel that income they get is commensurate with their contribution, they will be satisfied. Thus there is positive relationship between total family annual income and job satisfaction. Table 5.10 shows distribution of sample employees according to income and job satisfaction.

It can be observed from table 5.10 that the majority (56.82 per cent) of respondents with annual income Rs. 1.5 – 2.0 lakhs have high job satisfaction group, 46.81 per cent of respondents with income between Rs. 1.5 – 2.0 lakhs, 14.89 per cent of respondents with income below Rs.1.5 lakhs, and 26.24 per cent of respondents with income between Rs.2 – 2.5 lakhs fall in moderate satisfaction group and the majority (79.41 per cent) of respondents, irrespective of their income levels, belong to low satisfaction group. The chi-square value is given by 17.551 which is highly significant at 1 per cent level. It reveals that there is significant association between total family annual income and job satisfaction. The null hypothesis formulated for job satisfaction is rejected.

Table 5.10
Total Family Annual Income and Level of Job Satisfaction

(N = 360)

Level of Job satisfaction	Total Family Annual Income				Total	Chi-square
	Below Rs.1, 50,000	Rs.1, 50,001 – Rs. 2,00,000	Rs. 2,00,001 – Rs. 2,50,000	Rs. 2,50,001 Above		
High	6 (13.64)	25 (56.82)	6 (13.64)	7 (15.91)	44 (100)	
Moderate	42 (14.89)	132 (46.81)	74 (26.24)	34 (12.06)	282 (100)	$\chi2 = 17.551$ ** DF= 4
Low	4 (11.76)	27 (79.41)	3 (8.82)	0 (.00)	34 (100)	
Total	**52 (14.44)**	**184 (51.11)**	**83 (23.06)**	**41 (11.39)**	**360 (100)**	

Source: Field Survey
Note : Figures in parenthesis are percentages to respective column totals
    ** Significant at 0.01 per cent level

Educational Qualification and Level of Job Satisfaction

Table 5.11 demonstrates the details of educational qualification of respondents and job satisfaction. It is that, the majority respondents (31.82 per cent) of employees are graduates, 11.36 per cent of respondents have professional degree and 25 per cent of respondents have a P.G qualification. All of them belong to the high level of satisfaction group whereas 45.39 per cent respondents, with below 10th class qualification, fall in the moderate satisfaction groups. The chi-square value is given by 23.135 which is highly significant at 1 per cent level. It reveals that there is significant association between educational qualification and level of job satisfaction. The null hypothesis formulated for job satisfaction is rejected.

Table 5.11
Educational Qualification and Level of Job Satisfaction

(N = 360)

Level of Job Satisfaction	Educational Qualifications						Chi-square
	Below 10th	Inter	Graduate	Post Graduate	Professionals	Total	
High	11 (25.00)	3 (6.82)	14 (31.82)	11 (25.00)	5 (11.36)	44 (100)	
Moderate	128 (45.39)	17 (6.03)	68 (24.11)	49 (17.38)	20 (7.09)	282 (100)	$\chi2 = 23.135$ **
Low	25 (73.53)	3 (8.82)	6 (17.65)	0 (.00)	0 (.00)	34 (100)	DF= 8
Total	**164** **(45.56)**	**23** **(6.39)**	**88** **(24.44)**	**60** **(16.67)**	**25** **(6.94)**	**360** **(100)**	

Source: Field Survey

Note : Figures in parenthesis are percentages to respective column totals

** Significant at 0.01 per cent level

Technical Qualification and Level of Job Satisfaction

Table 5.12 shows the relationship between technical qualification and job satisfaction. Most of the respondents with no technical qualification belong to high, moderate and low job satisfaction groups. The chi-square value is given by 16.354which is significant at 5 per cent level. It reveals that there is significant association between technical qualification and job satisfaction. The null hypothesis formulated for job satisfaction is rejected.

Table 5.12
Technical Qualification and Level of Job Satisfaction

(N = 360)

Level of Job satisfaction	Technical Qualification						Chi-Square
	No Technical Qualification	Typing	DCA	PGDCA	B.Tech	Total	
High	28 (63.64)	4 (9.09)	3 (6.82)	8 (18.18)	1 (2.27)	44 (100)	
Moderate	216 (76.60)	30 (10.64)	10 (3.55)	22 (7.80)	4 (1.42)	282 (100)	$\chi^2 = 16.354^*$
Low	33 (97.06)	0 (0.00)	1 (2.94)	0 (0.00)	0 (0.00)	34 (100)	DF = 8
Total	277 (76.94)	34 (9.44)	14 (3.89)	30 (8.33)	5 (1.39)	360 (100)	

Source: Field Survey

Note : Figures in parenthesis are percentages to respective column totals
*Significant at 0.05 levels.

Monthly Salary and Level of Job Satisfaction

Details of monthly salary and job satisfaction are presented in table 5.13. It can be noted from the table that majority (47.73 per cent) of the respondents with monthly income Rs. 10,000 – 15, 000, (22.73 per cent) of respondents with monthly income below 10,000 belong to are high satisfaction groups, majority (10.28 per cent) of respondents with monthly income above 20,000 fall in the moderate satisfaction group, and 50 per cent of respondents with monthly income ranging between Rs. 15,000 – 20,000 fall in the low satisfaction group. The chi- square value is not significant. So, it implies that there is no association between monthly salary and job satisfaction; hence, the null hypothesis is accepted.

Table 5.13
Monthly Salary and Level of Job Satisfaction

(N = 360)

Level of Job satisfaction	Monthly Salary					Chi-square
	Below Rs. 10,000	Rs.10001 – Rs.15000	Rs.15001- Rs.20, 000	Above 20,000	Total	
High	10 (22.73)	21 (47.73)	12 (27.27)	1 (2.27)	44 (100)	χ2 = 11.151 NS DF= 6
Moderate	49 (17.38)	112 (39.72)	92 (32.62)	29 (10.28)	282 (100)	
Low	6 (17.65)	11 (32.35)	17 (50.00)	0 (0.00)	34 (100)	
Total	65 (18.06)	144 (40.00)	121 (33.61)	30 (8.33)	360 (100)	

Source: Field Survey
Note : Figures in parenthesis are percentages to respective column totals
NS : Not significant at 5 per cent level

No. Of Years Service and Level of Job Satisfaction

Several investigations have revealed that there is a positive relationship between number of years service and job satisfaction. Employees with greater experience tend to be more satisfied with their jobs. This is because of their better adjustment to work situation stemming from experience with it. The lengths of service in the organization broadness the knowledge of the employees about the organization and develop a sort of loyalty and attachment to the concern. Table 5.14 shows relationship between number of years of service and level of job satisfaction.

It is observed from table 5.14 majority (25 per cent) of respondents having service ranging from 16 to 20 years have high satisfaction, whereas employees (30.14 per cent) having service ranging from 11- 15 years have moderate satisfaction and majority (61.76 per cent) of respondents having service ranging from 20 years and above fall in the low satisfaction group. The chi-square value is 38.206 which is highly significant at 1 per cent level. It reveals that there is significant association between number of years of service and job satisfaction. The null hypothesis formulated for job satisfaction is rejected.

Table 5.14
No. Of Years Service and Level of Job Satisfaction

(N = 360)

Level of Job Satisfaction	No. of Years in TTD						Chi-square
	Below 5	6 -10	11- 15	16-20	20 & Above	Total	
High	7 (15.91)	9 (20.45)	7 (15.91)	11 (25.00)	10 (22.73)	44 (100)	
Moderate	39 (13.83)	28 (9.93)	85 (30.14)	75 (26.60)	55 (19.50)	282 (100)	$\chi2 = 38.206$ ** DF= 8
Low	2 (5.88)	1 (2.94)	3 (8.82)	7 (20.59)	21 (61.76)	34 (100)	
Total	48 (13.33)	38 (10.56)	95 (26.39)	93 (25.83)	86 (23.89)	360 (100)	

Source: Field Survey
Note : Figures in parenthesis are percentages to respective column totals
      ** Significant at 0.01 per cent level

Promotions and Level of Job Satisfaction

Promotion is an advancement of an employee to a better job, better in terms of greater responsibilities, more prestige, and greater skills. Hence, it significantly affects job satisfaction. Table 5.15 shows relationship between number of promotions received so far and job satisfaction. It is observed from the table 5.15 that 27 respondents who have not received any promotions (61.36 per cent) are in high satisfaction group, whereas, most of the respondents (73.40 per cent, and 88.24 per cent) who have not received any promotions belong to the moderate and low satisfaction groups. Chi-square values computed in this regard are found to be not significant. But, there is no significant relationship between number of promotions received and job satisfaction. Hence, the null hypothesis is accepted.

148

Table 5.15

Promotions and Level of Job Satisfaction

(N = 360)

Level of Job Satisfaction	No. of Promotions received sofar in TTD						Chi-square
	Nil	Once	Twice	Three Times	Four & Above	Total	
High	27 (61.36)	11 (25.00)	6 (13.64)	0 (0.00)	0 (0.00)	44 (100)	χ2 = 9.112 NS DF= 6
Moderate	207 (73.40)	55 (19.50)	19 (6.74)	1 (0.35)	0 (0.00)	282 (100)	
Low	30 (88.24)	4 (11.76)	0 (0.00)	0 (0.00)	0 (0.00)	34 (100)	
Total	264 (73.33)	70 (19.44)	25 (6.94)	1 0.28)	0 (0.00)	360 (100)	

Source: Field Survey

Note : Figures in parenthesis are percentages to respective column totals

NS   : Not significant at 5 per cent level

Awards and Rewards and Level of Job Satisfaction

From table 5.16, it is explicitly found that there is a definite relation between job satisfaction and awards and rewards received by the employees in the present study. However, more than 98 per cent of the respondents have not received any kind of awards and rewards in TTD. The chi-square value is not significant. It can be concluded that there is no relationship between no. of awards and rewards received and job Satisfaction. The hypothesis formulated is accepted.

149

Table 5.16
Awards and Rewards and Level of Job Satisfaction

(N = 360)

Level of Job Satisfaction	No. of Awards & Rewards				Chi-square
	Not Received	Monetary	Non-Monetary	Total	
High	44 (100.00)	0 (00)	0 (00)	44 (100)	$\chi 2 = 1.688$ NS DF= 4
Moderate	276 (97.87)	4 (1.42)	2 (0.71)	282 (100)	
Low	34 (100.00)	0 (00)	0 (00)	34 (100)	
Total	**354** **(98.33)**	**4** **(1.11)**	**2** **(0.56)**	**360** **(100)**	

Source: Field Survey

Note : Figures in parenthesis are percentages to respective column totals

NS : Not significant at 5 per cent level

Training Programmes Attended and Level of Job Satisfaction

Table 5.17 reveals an association between employees' training programmes attended and the felt job satisfaction. Majority (29.55 per cent) of the respondents who attended training programmes once perceived high satisfaction level. 48.94per cent of the respondents who had not attended training programmes fall in moderate satisfaction level, whereas, 47.06 per cent of the respondents who attended training programmes once fall in low satisfaction levels. The chi-square value is given by 57.699which is highly significant at 1 per cent level. It reveals that there is significant association between training programmes and job satisfaction. The null hypothesis formulated for job satisfaction is rejected.

Table 5.17
Training Programmes attended and Level of Job satisfaction

(N = 360)

Level of Job Satisfaction	Training Programmes						Chi-Square
	Not Attended	One Time	Two Times	Three Times	Four Times & Above	Total	
High	5 (11.36)	13 (29.55)	9 (20.45)	5 (11.36)	12 (27.27)	44 (100)	
Moderate	138 (48.94)	51 (18.09)	15 (5.32)	28 (9.93)	50 (17.73)	282 (100)	$\chi^2 = 57.699$
Low	2 (5.88)	16 (47.06)	0 (0.00)	6 (17.65)	10 (29.41)	34 (100)	**
Total	145 (40.28)	80 (22.22)	24 (6.67)	39 (10.83)	72 (20.00)	360 (100)	DF= 8

Source: Field Survey

Note : Figures in parenthesis are percentages to respective column totals
** Significant at 0.01 per cent level

Aspects of Job Satisfaction

Table 5.18 reveals that the mean score values are in the range of 2.65 and 4.06 indicating that most of the respondents are satisfied with their jobs. In fact, six factors viz., administrative policies of the TTD, superior-subordinate relationship, authority and responsibility being enjoyed on the job, scope for future growth and development in life as an employee in TTD, transfer policy, and promotional avenues are dissatisfaction factors. The researcher assumed that mean score below 3.50 is in dissatisfaction aspect.

Table 5.18
Dimensions of job satisfaction

(N = 360)

S. No	Job factors	Score Value	Mean (X)	S.D	C.V
1	Being an employee in TTD	1462	4.06	0.83	20.41
2	The present position in TTD	1305	3.63	0.79	21.71
3	Nature of job currently doing	1298	3.61	0.84	23.33
4	Salary being drawn on the current job	1366	3.79	0.89	23.56
5	Salary in relation to nature of job	1326	3.68	0.94	25.63
6	Salary in relation to experience on the job	1346	3.74	0.88	23.43
7	Salary in relation to educational qualification	1348	3.74	0.86	22.92
8	Salary that is being paid in TTD compared to the same cadre in other organizations	1327	3.69	0.99	26.85
9	Administrative policies of the TTD	1162	3.23	1.02	31.59
10	Superior-Subordinate relationship	1242	3.45	1.05	30.56
11	Working relationships among the colleagues	1286	3.57	0.86	24.19
12	Overall working condition in TTD	1261	3.50	0.84	24.11
13	The job status being enjoyed in TTD	1328	3.69	0.87	23.47
14	Work Achievement drive on the job being performed	1293	3.59	0.88	24.63
15	Authority and responsibility being enjoyed on the job	1113	3.09	1.06	34.23
16	Scope for future growth and development in life as an employee in TTD	1058	2.94	1.17	39.86
17	Recognition being enjoyed in the society as an employee in TTD.	1271	3.53	1.10	31.20
18	Retirement Benefits	1310	3.64	0.96	26.31
19	Transfer Policy	1102	3.06	1.04	34.08
20	Promotional Avenues	954	2.65	1.16	43.72

Job Satisfaction Factors with Gender

Table 5.19 furnishes the ANOVA results of F-test for each dimension across the male and female employees. Under each male and female, mean is calculated for each dimension of job satisfaction and F-test is done for each job satisfaction dimension across gender to know the statistically significant differences. Statistically significant differences are found in respect of 9 out of 20 items.

They are: Salary being drawn on the current job, salary that is being paid in TTD compared to the salary paid to the same cadre in other organization, working relationships among the colleagues, overall working condition in TTD, the job status being enjoyed in TTD, authority and responsibility being enjoyed on the job, scope for future growth and development in life as an employee in TTD, recognition being enjoyed in the society as an employee of TTD, retirement benefits and Promotional Avenues.

Table 5.19
Results of ANOVA for Job Satisfaction Factors with Gender

(N = 360)

Sl. No.	Job Factors		Sum of Squares	Degrees of Freedom	Mean Square	F-Ratio	Mean For Gender	
							Male	Female
1	2	3	4	5	6	7	8	9
1	Being an employee in TTD	Effect	0.118	1	0.118	0.172NS	4.05	4.09
		Error	246.537	358	0.689			
		Total	246.656	359				
2	The present position in TTD	Effect	0.675	1	0.675	1.090NS	3.65	3.56
		Error	221.700	358	0.619			
		Total	222.375	359				
3	Nature of job currently doing	Effect	1.275	1	1.275	1.806NS	3.57	3.69
		Error	252.714	358	0.706			
		Total	253.989	359				
4	Salary being drawn on the current job	Effect	5.897	1	5.897	7.516**	3.71	3.98
		Error	280.892	358	0.785			
		Total	286.789	359				
5	Salary in relation to nature of job	Effect	0.046	1	0.046	0.052NS	3.69	3.67
		Error	319.854	358	0.893			
		Total	319.900	359				

1	2	3	4	5	6	7	8	9
6	Salary in relation to experience on the job	Effect	1.488	1	1.488	1.945NS	3.70	3.83
		Error	273.967	358	0.765			
		Total	275.456	359				
7	Salary in relation to educational qualification	Effect	0.045	1	0.045	0.061NS	3.75	3.73
		Error	264.444	358	0.739			
		Total	264.489	359				
8	Salary that is being paid in TTD Compared to the same cadre in other	Effect	19.309	1	19.309	20.807**	3.53	4.03
		Error	332.222	358	0.928			
		Total	351.531	359				
9	Administrative policies of the TTD	Effect	1.292	1	1.292	1.244NS	3.19	3.32
		Error	372.030	358	1.039			
		Total	373.322	359				
10	Superior-Subordinate relationship	Effect	1.208	1	1.208	1.087NS	3.41	3.54
		Error	397.892	358	1.111			
		Total	399.100	359				
11	Working relationships among the colleagues	Effect	2.979	1	2.979	4.022*	3.63	3.44
		Error	265.143	358	0.741			
		Total	268.122	359				
12	Overall working condition in TTD	Effect	6.605	1	6.605	9.481**	3.41	3.70
		Error	249.392	358	0.697			
		Total	255.997	359				
13	The job status being enjoyed in TTD	Effect	7.069	1	7.069	9.656**	3.59	3.89
		Error	262.086	358	0.732			
		Total	269.156	359				
14	Work Achievement drive on the job being performed	Effect	0.077	1	0.077	0.098NS	3.60	3.57
		Error	280.898	358	0.785			
		Total	280.975	359				
15	Authority and responsibility being enjoyed on the job	Effect	10.390	1	10.390	9.499**	3.21	2.84
		Error	391.585	358	1.094			
		Total	401.975	359				
16	Scope for future growth and development in life as an employee in TTD	Effect	17.605	1	17.605	13.268**	3.09	2.61
		Error	475.050	358	1.327			
		Total	492.656	359				

1	2	3	4	5	6	7	8	9
17	Recognition being enjoyed in the society as an employee	Effect	9.026	1	9.026	7.574**	3.42	3.76
		Error	426.638	358	1.192			
		Total	435.664	359				
18	Retirement Benefits	Effect	7.497	1	7.497	8.347**	3.54	3.85
		Error	321.558	358	0.898			
		Total	329.056	359				
19	Transfer Policy	Effect	0.457	1	0.457	0.419NS	3.09	3.01
		Error	390.199	358	1.090			
		Total	390.656	359				
20	Promotional Avenues	Effect	16.729	1	16.729	12.875**	2.80	2.33
		Error	465.171	358	1.299			
		Total	481.900	359				

Note: **Significant at 1 per cent level
*Significant at 5 per cent level.
NS : Not significant

5.20 Job Satisfaction Factors with Age group

Table 5.20 furnishes the ANOVA results of F-test for each dimension across the three age groups viz., lower age (< 30 years), moderate age (30 years to 35 years) and higher age (35 years and above). Under each age group means are calculated for each dimension of job satisfaction and   F-test is done for each job satisfaction dimension across age to know the statistically significant differences. Statistically significant differences are found in respect of 10 out of 20 items.

They are: Salary being drawn on the current job, salary that is being paid in TTD compared to salary paid the same cadre in other organization, working relationships among the colleagues, overall working condition in TTD, the job status being enjoyed in TTD, authority and responsibility being enjoyed on the job, scope for future growth and development in life as an employee of TTD, recognition being enjoyed in the society as an employee of TTD, retirement benefits and promotional avenues.

Table 5.20
Results of ANOVA for Job Satisfaction Factors with Age Group

(N = 360)

Sl. No.	Job Factors		Sum of Squares	D.F	Mean Square	F-Ratio	Mean for Age		
							>35 Years	36 - 45	< 46 Years
1	2	3	4	5	6	7	8	9	10
1	Being an employee in TTD	Effect	4.765	2	2.383	3.516*	4.00	4.21	3.96
		Error	241.890	357	0.678				
		Total	246.656	359					
2	The present position in TTD	Effect	6.681	2	3.341	5.529**	3.74	3.73	3.45
		Error	215.694	357	0.604				
		Total	222.375	359					
3	Nature o job currently doing	Effect	9.245	2	4.622	6.743**	3.82	3.66	3.42
		Error	244.744	357	0.686				
		Total	253.989	359					
4	Salary being drawn on the current job	Effect	.442	2	0.221	0.275NS	3.79	3.84	3.76
		Error	286.347	357	0.802				
		Total	286.789	359					
5	Salary in relation to nature of job	Effect	2.189	2	1.095	1.230NS	3.68	3.78	3.60
		Error	317.711	357	0.890				
		Total	319.900	359					
6	Salary in relation to experience on the job	Effect	2.309	2	1.155	1.509NS	3.62	3.83	3.73
		Error	273.147	357	0.765				
		Total	275.456	359					
7	Salary in relation to educational qualification	Effect	2.821	2	1.411	1.925NS	3.80	3.82	3.63
		Error	261.667	357	0.733				
		Total	264.489	359					
8	Salary that is being paid in TTD Compared to the same cadre in other organizations	Effect	3.630	2	1.815	1.862NS	3.68	3.81	3.58
		Error	347.901	357	0.975				
		Total	351.531	359					
9	Administrative policies of the TTD	Effect	24.972	2	12.486	12.796**	3.62	3.27	2.94
		Error	348.351	357	0.976				
		Total	373.322	359					

1	2	3	4	5	6	7	8	9	10
10	Superior-Subordinate relationship	Effect	12.275	2	6.137	5.664**	3.74	3.25	3.46
		Error	386.825	357	1.084				
		Total	399.100	359					
11	Working relationships among the colleagues	Effect	2.862	2	1.431	1.926NS	3.59	3.67	3.47
		Error	265.260	357	0.743				
		Total	268.122	359					
12	Overall orking condition in TTD	Effect	14.700	2	7.350	10.875**	3.45	3.75	3.29
		Error	241.297	357	0.676				
		Total	255.997	359					
13	The job status being enjoyed in TTD	Effect	20.263	2	10.132	14.532**	3.76	3.94	3.40
		Error	248.892	357	0.697				
		Total	269.156	359					
14	Work Achievement drive on the job being performed	Effect	25.632	2	12.816	17.918**	4.03	3.56	3.35
		Error	255.343	357	0.715				
		Total	280.975	359					
15	Authority and responsibility being enjoyed on the job	Effect	27.776	2	13.888	13.250**	3.48	3.16	2.78
		Error	374.199	357	1.048				
		Total	401.975	359					
16	Scope for future growth and development in life as an employee in	Effect	59.978	2	29.989	24.744**	3.64	2.82	2.61
		Error	432.677	357	1.212				
		Total	492.656	359					
17	Recognition being enjoyed in the society as an employee in TTD	Effect	17.705	2	8.852	7.561**	3.68	3.72	3.25
		Error	417.959	357	1.171				
		Total	435.664	359					
18	Retirement Benefits	Effect	22.822	2	11.411	13.303**	3.74	3.90	3.33
		Error	306.234	357	0.858				
		Total	329.056	359					
19	Transfer Policy	Effect	24.139	2	12.069	11.756**	3.52	2.95	2.88
		Error	366.517	357	1.027				
		Total	390.656	359					
20	Promotional Avenues	Effect	67.812	2	33.906	29.232**	3.40	2.51	2.31
		Error	414.088	357	1.160				
		Total	481.900	359					

Note : **Significant at 1 per cent level, *significant at 5 per cent level,

N.S : Not significant

5.21 Job Satisfaction Factors with Education

On the basis of ANOVA results for educational level, respondents were divided into three viz., highly educated (post graduate and above), moderately educated (graduates) and low education (intermediate and below) levels. F-test is done for each job satisfaction dimension across educational levels to know the statistically significant differences (table 5.21). Statistically significant differences are found in respect of 13 out of 19 items. They are:

The present position in TTD, nature of job currently doing, salary in relation to nature of job, salary in relation to educational qualification, administrative policies of the TTD, superior-subordinate relationship, overall working condition in TTD, the job status being enjoyed in TTD, work achievement drive on the job being performed, authority and responsibility being enjoyed on the job, scope for future growth and development in life as an employee of TTD, recognition being enjoyed in the society as an employee of TTD, retirement benefits and Promotional Avenues. The results indicate that higher educated respondents have a higher level of job satisfaction when compared to the graduates and respondents with intermediate qualification.

Table 5.21
Results of ANOVA for Job Satisfaction Factors with Education

(N = 360)

Sl. No.	Job Factors		Sum of Squares	D.F	Mean Square	F-Ratio	Mean for Education		
							High	Mode rate	Low
1	2	3	4	5	6	7	8	9	10
1	Being an employee in TTD	Effect	2.227	2	1.113	1.626NS	4.01	4.21	4.04
		Error	244.429	357	0.685				
		Total	246.656	359					
2	The present position in TTD	Effect	6.947	2	3.473	5.756**	3.54	3.57	3.89
		Error	215.428	357	0.603				
		Total	222.375	359					
3	Nature of job currently doing	Effect	8.629	2	4.315	6.278**	3.48	3.72	3.84
		Error	245.359	357	0.687				
		Total	253.989	359					
4	Salary being drawn on the current job	Effect	3.770	2	1.885	2.378NS	3.74	3.75	3.99
		Error	283.019	357	0.793				
		Total	286.789	359					
5	Salary in relation to nature of job	Effect	9.027	2	4.513	5.183**	3.58	3.67	3.97
		Error	310.873	357	0.871				
		Total	319.900	359					
6	Salary in relation to experience on the job	Effect	1.938	2	0.969	1.265NS	3.69	3.73	3.87
		Error	273.517	357	0.766				
		Total	275.456	359					
7	Salary in relation to educational qualification	Effect	7.332	2	3.666	5.089**	3.62	3.89	3.92
		Error	257.157	357	0.720				
		Total	264.489	359					
8	Salary that is being paid in TTD Compared to the same cadre in other organizations	Effect	.545	2	0.273	0.277NS	3.67	3.67	3.76
		Error	350.985	357	0.983				
		Total	351.531	359					
9	Administrative policies of the TTD	Effect	14.960	2	7.480	7.452**	3.07	3.31	3.57
		Error	358.362	357	1.004				
		Total	373.322	359					
10	Superior-Subordinate relationship	Effect	7.502	2	3.751	3.420*	3.41	3.29	3.71
		Error	391.598	357	1.097				
		Total	399.100	359					

1	2	3	4	5	6	7	8	9	10
11	Working relationships among the colleagues	Effect	1.830	2	0.915	1.227NS			
		Error	266.292	357	0.746		3.52	3.71	3.57
		Total	268.122	359					
12	Overall working condition in TTD	Effect	7.962	2	3.981	5.730**			
		Error	248.035	357	0.695		3.50	3.73	3.28
		Total	255.997	359					
13	The job status being enjoyed in TTD	Effect	6.291	2	3.145	4.272*			
		Error	262.865	357	0.736		3.59	3.92	3.73
		Total	269.156	359					
14	Work Achievement drive on the job being performed	Effect	43.517	2	21.758	32.712**			
		Error	237.458	357	0.665		3.29	3.97	4.01
		Total	280.975	359					
15	Authority and responsibility being enjoyed on the job	Effect	68.481	2	34.240	36.654**			
		Error	333.494	357	0.934		2.73	3.36	3.77
		Total	401.975	359					
16	Scope for future growth and development in life as an employee in TTD	Effect	130.849	2	65.425	64.556**			
		Error	361.806	357	1.013		2.47	3.17	3.95
		Total	492.656	359					
17	Recognition being enjoyed in the society as an employee in TTD	Effect	19.475	2	9.738	8.353**			
		Error	416.189	357	1.166		3.34	3.64	3.91
		Total	435.664	359					
18	Retirement Benefits	Effect	9.649	2	4.824	5.392**			
		Error	319.407	357	0.895		3.51	3.71	3.91
		Total	329.056	359					
19	Transfer Policy	Effect	64.929	2	32.464	35.581**			
		Error	325.727	357	0.912		2.72	3.28	3.75
		Total	390.656	359					
20	Promotional Avenues	Effect	107.862	2	53.931	51.474**			
		Error	374.038	357	1.048		2.20	2.96	3.52
		Total	481.900	359					

Note : **Significant at 1 per cent level
* significant at 5 per cent level,
NS : Not significant

160

5.22 Job Satisfaction Factors with Monthly Salary

ANOVA result indicates there is significant difference in the perception on job satisfaction across the income levels of respondents; the perceptions are tabulated in table 5. 22 across different income groups. Income groups are classified into lower income (up to Rs. 10,000), moderate income (Rs. 10,001 to Rs. 20,000) and higher income (more than Rs. 20.00) groups. Under each income group means were calculated for each dimension of job satisfaction. F-test is done for each job satisfaction dimension across income levels to know the statistically significant differences. Statistically significant differences are found in respect of 12 out of 20 items. They are: Being Employee in TTD, the present position in TTD, nature of present job, overall working conditions in TTD, the job status being enjoyed in TTD, work Achievement drive on the job being performed, authority and responsibility being enjoyed on the job, scope for future growth and development in life as an employee of TTD, recognition being enjoyed in the society as an employee of TTD retirement benefits,   transfer policy and promotional Avenues, Therefore, it can be said that monthly salary has an influence on the perception on job satisfaction

Table 5.22
Results of ANOVA for Job Satisfaction Factors with Monthly Salary

(N = 360)

Sl. No.	Job Factors		Sum of Squares	D.F	Mean Square	F-Ratio	Mean for Salary		
							> 10,000	10 - 20	< 20,000
1	2	3	4	5	6	7	8	9	10
1	Being an employee in TTD	Effect	6.614	2	3.307	4.919**	4.03	3.93	4.27
		Error	240.041	357	0.672				
		Total	246.656	359					
2	The present position in TTD	Effect	7.141	2	3.570	5.922**	3.67	3.44	3.79
		Error	215.234	357	0.603				
		Total	222.375	359					
3	Nature of job currently doing	Effect	7.358	2	3.679	5.325**	3.72	3.40	3.69
		Error	246.631	357	0.691				
		Total	253.989	359					
4	Salary being drawn on the current job	Effect	1.492	2	0.746	0.933NS	3.87	3.72	3.78
		Error	285.297	357	0.799				
		Total	286.789	359					
5	Salary in relation to nature of job	Effect	2.698	2	1.349	1.518NS	3.78	3.59	3.65
		Error	317.202	357	0.889				
		Total	319.900	359					
6	Salary in relation to experience on the job	Effect	1.531	2	0.766	0.998NS	3.81	3.74	3.64
		Error	273.924	357	0.767				
		Total	275.456	359					
7	Salary in relation to educational qualification	Effect	2.497	2	1.249	1.702NS	3.81	3.63	3.79
		Error	261.991	357	0.734				
		Total	264.489	359					
8	Salary that is being paid in TTD Compared to the same cadre in other organizations	Effect	3.727	2	1.863	1.913NS	3.80	3.66	3.55
		Error	347.804	357	0.974				
		Total	351.531	359					
9	Administrative policies of the TTD	Effect	5.473	2	2.736	2.656NS	3.17	3.13	3.43
		Error	367.849	357	1.030				
		Total	373.322	359					
10	Superior-Subordinate relationship	Effect	.408	2	0.204	0.183NS	3.42	3.44	3.51
		Error	398.692	357	1.117				
		Total	399.100	359					
11	Working relationships among the colleagues	Effect	1.699	2	0.849	1.138NS	3.65	3.50	3.55
		Error	266.424	357	0.746				
		Total	268.122	359					

1	2	3	4	5	6	7	8	9	10
12	Overall working condition in TTD	Effect	19.583	2	9.792	14.786**	3.62	3.18	3.74
		Error	236.414	357	0.662				
		Total	255.997	359					
13	The job status being enjoyed in TTD	Effect	45.462	2	22.731	36.278**	3.92	3.19	3.97
		Error	223.693	357	0.627				
		Total	269.156	359					
14	Work Achievement drive on the job being performed	Effect	23.480	2	11.740	16.277**	3.49	3.38	4.01
		Error	257.495	357	0.721				
		Total	280.975	359					
15	Authority and responsibility being enjoyed on the job	Effect	36.973	2	18.486	18.081**	3.08	2.74	3.57
		Error	365.002	357	1.022				
		Total	401.975	359					
16	Scope for future growth and development in life as an employee in TTD	Effect	35.914	2	17.957	14.036**	2.94	2.58	3.40
		Error	456.742	357	1.279				
		Total	492.656	359					
17	Recognition being enjoyed in the society as an employee in TTD	Effect	27.051	2	13.525	11.817**	3.65	3.16	3.82
		Error	408.613	357	1.145				
		Total	435.664	359					
18	Retirement Benefits	Effect	16.560	2	8.280	9.459**	3.84	3.35	3.71
		Error	312.495	357	0.875				
		Total	329.056	359					
19	Transfer Policy	Effect	13.547	2	6.773	6.412**	3.06	2.84	3.35
		Error	377.109	357	1.056				
		Total	390.656	359					
20	Promotional Avenues	Effect	60.977	2	30.489	25.859**	2.49	2.31	3.33
		Error	420.923	357	1.179				
		Total	481.900	359					

Note : **Significant at 1 per cent level
*significant at 5 per cent level,

NS : Not significant

5.23 Job Satisfaction Factors with Experience

Table 5.23 examines the results of ANOVA for influence of experience on the perceptions of respondents. Based on length of service three groups are formed. They are: low (up to 10 years), medium (10 years to 15 years) and high (more than 16 years) groups. F-test is done for each job satisfaction dimension across experience to know the statistically significant differences. Statistically significant differences are found in respect of 12 out of 20 items. They are: Nature of job, administrative policies of the TTD, superior-subordinate relationship, overall working conditions in TTD, the job status being enjoyed in TTD, work Achievement drive on the job being performed, authority and responsibility being enjoyed on the job, scope for future growth and development in life as an employee of TTD, recognition being enjoyed in the society as an employee of TTD, retirement benefits, transfer policy and promotional avenues. Therefore, work experience does not affect the perceptions of the respondents.

Table 5.23
Results of ANOVA for Job Satisfaction Factors with Experience

(N = 360)

Sl. No.	Job Factors		Sum of Squares	D.F	Mean Square	F-Ratio	Mean for Experience		
							>10 Years	11–15 Years	< 16 Years
1	2	3	4	5	6	7	8	9	10
1	Being an employee in TTD	Effect	0.361	2	0.181	0.262NS	4.10	4.08	4.03
		Error	246.294	357	0.690				
		Total	246.656	359					
2	The present position in TTD	Effect	2.317	2	1.158	1.879NS	3.76	3.55	3.60
		Error	220.058	357	0.616				
		Total	222.375	359					
3	Nature of job currently doing	Effect	20.867	2	10.433	15.977**	3.81	3.86	3.35
		Error	233.122	357	0.653				
		Total	253.989	359					
4	Salary being drawn on the current job	Effect	1.357	2	0.678	0.849NS	3.78	3.89	3.74
		Error	285.432	357	0.800				
		Total	286.789	359					
5	Salary in relation to nature of job	Effect	0.305	2	0.152	0.170NS	3.67	3.73	3.66
		Error	319.595	357	0.895				
		Total	319.900	359					

1	2	3	4	5	6	7	8	9	10
6	Salary in relation to experience on the job	Effect	1.696	2	0.848	1.106NS	3.63	3.81	3.76
		Error	273.759	357	0.767				
		Total	275.456	359					
7	Salary in relation to educational qualification	Effect	0.354	2	0.177	0.239NS	3.80	3.71	3.74
		Error	264.135	357	0.740				
		Total	264.489	359					
8	Salary that is being paid in TTD Compared to the same cadre in other organizations	Effect	2.706	2	1.353	1.385NS	3.70	3.81	3.60
		Error	348.824	357	0.977				
		Total	351.531	359					
9	Administrative policies of the TTD	Effect	22.270	2	11.135	11.324**	3.66	3.15	3.05
		Error	351.052	357	0.983				
		Total	373.322	359					
10	Superior-Subordinate relationship	Effect	25.598	2	12.799	12.233**	3.91	3.22	3.35
		Error	373.502	357	1.046				
		Total	399.100	359					
11	Working relationships among the colleagues	Effect	1.734	2	0.867	1.162NS	3.50	3.68	3.55
		Error	266.388	357	0.746				
		Total	268.122	359					
12	Overall working condition in TTD	Effect	4.790	2	2.395	3.404*	3.70	3.42	3.45
		Error	251.207	357	0.704				
		Total	255.997	359					
13	The job status being enjoyed in TTD	Effect	12.121	2	6.060	8.417**	3.95	3.76	3.51
		Error	257.035	357	0.720				
		Total	269.156	359					
14	Work Achievement drive on the job being performed	Effect	41.924	2	20.962	31.305**	4.17	3.54	3.33
		Error	239.051	357	0.670				
		Total	280.975	359					
15	Authority and responsibility being enjoyed on the job	Effect	24.867	2	12.434	11.771**	3.51	2.79	3.05
		Error	377.108	357	1.056				
		Total	401.975	359					
16	Scope for future growth and development in life as an employee in TTD	Effect	55.176	2	27.588	22.513**	3.63	2.67	2.74
		Error	437.479	357	1.225				
		Total	492.656	359					

1	2	3	4	5	6	7	8	9	10
17	Recognition being enjoyed in the society as an employee in TTD	Effect	23.887	2	11.943	10.355**	3.85	3.70	3.27
		Error	411.777	357	1.153				
		Total	435.664	359					
18	Retirement Benefits	Effect	12.638	2	6.319	7.130**	3.90	3.73	3.45
		Error	316.417	357	0.886				
		Total	329.056	359					
19	Transfer Policy	Effect	32.006	2	16.003	15.929**	3.58	2.96	2.85
		Error	358.649	357	1.005				
		Total	390.656	359					
20	Promotional Avenues	Effect	47.499	2	23.750	19.518**	3.27	2.57	2.38
		Error	434.401	357	1.217				
		Total	481.900	359					

Note : **Significant at 1 per cent level
*Significant at 5 per cent level,
NS : Not significant

5.24 Correlation Analysis

To examine further the validity of the hypothesis, correlations between the personal variables such as age, gender, income, education and experience and perceptions of employees' job satisfaction scores are found. Table 5.24 shows the respondent's job satisfaction and its relationship with age, gender, income, education and experience variables. It is found that significant correlation at 0.05 level with about 12 of the dimensions and also with overall climate. However, the coefficients are negative and below 0.01 indicating a low job satisfaction relationship.

Table 5.24
Correlation between Job factors and Personnel Variables

(N = 360)

S. No	Job Factors	Age	Gender	Monthly Salary	Education	Experience
1	2	3	4	5	6	7
1	Being an employee in TTD	-0.040	0.022	-0.082	0.017	-0.038
2	The present position in TTD	-0.152*	-0.055	-0.031	0.182**	-0.071
3	Nature of job currently doing	-0.189**	0.071	-0.012	0.187**	-0.246**
4	Salary being drawn on the current job	-0.021	0.143**	0.017	0.073	-0.029
5	Salary in relation to nature of job	-0.044	-0.012	-0.035	0.139**	-0.009
6	Salary in relation to experience on the job	0.035	0.073	0.008	0.053	0.050
7	Salary in relation to educational qualification	-0.086*	-0.013	-0.106*	0.127**	-0.022
8	Salary that is being paid in TTD compared to the	-0.053	0.234**	-0.051	0.000	-0.054
9	Administrative policies of the TTD	-0.259**	0.059	-0.087*	0.195**	-0.227**
10	Superior-subordinate relationship	-0.079	0.055	-0.016	0.095*	-0.187*
11	Working relationship among the colleagues	-0.065	-0.105*	-0.027	0.013	0.008
12	Overall working conditions in TTD	-0.102*	0.161**	-0.188**	-0.086*	-0.110**
13	The job status being enjoyed in TTD	-0.189**	0.162**	-0.208**	0.129**	-0.212**

167

1	2	3	4	5	6	7
14	Work achievement drive on the job being performed	-0.294**	-0.017	-0.093*	0.354**	-0.372**
15	Authority and responsibility being enjoyed on the job	-0.262**	-0.161**	-0.048	0.416**	-0.141**
16	Scope for future growth and development in life as an employees in TTD	-0.326**	-0.189**	-0.011	0.513**	-0.273**
17	Reorganization being enjoyed in the society as an employee in	-0.167**	0.144**	-0.019	0.232**	-0.227**
18	Retirement benefits	-0.191**	0.151**	-0.071	0.214**	-0.194**
19	Transfer policy	-0.220**	-0.034	0.049	0.409**	-0.265**
20	Promotional avenues	-0.348**	-0.186**	0.046	0.489**	-0.299**

Note : **Significant at 1 per cent level
*Significant at 5 per cent level,

NS : Not significant

5.25 Factor Analysis for Job Satisfaction

Table 5.25 shows the result of Factor analysis by principal components analysis method is applied on 20 variables of job satisfaction. They are then reduced to four major factors namely. Factor 1, factor 2, factor 3, and factor 4.

Factor 1 contained six attributes and explained 42.393 % of the variance in the data, with an eigen value of 8.479 and a reliability of 92.3 %.

Factor 2 accounted for 11.64 % of the variance, with an eigen value of 2.329 and a reliability of 83.5 %. This factor was loaded with 5 attributes.

Factor 3 was loaded with five attributes. This factor accounted for 8.536 % of the variance, with an eigen value of 1.707 and a reliability of 85.8 %.

Factor 4 contained four attributes that referred to job satisfaction aspects. This factor explained 85.8 % of the variance, with an eigen value of 1.455 and a reliability of 73.4.

Table: 5.25
Factor Analysis Results of Job Satisfaction Aspects

(N= 360)

Attributes	Factor Loading				Communality
	Factor 1	Factor 2	Factor 3	Factor 4	
Factor 1 :					
Salary in relation to educational qualification	**0.904**				0.881
Salary that is being paid in TTD compared to the same cadre in other org	**0.851**				0.797
Salary in relation to experience on the job	**0.835**				0.838
Salary in relation to nature of job	**0.809**				0.769
Salary being drawn on the current job	**0.788**				0.806
Administrative policies of the TTD	**0.636**				0.581
Factor 2 :					
Job status being enjoyed in TTD		**0.812**			0.733
Retirement benefits		**0.733**			0.682
Recognition being enjoyed in society as an employee in TTD		**0.689**			0.744
Work achievement drive on the job being performed		**0.671**			0.567
Overall working condition in TTD		**0.452**			0.488
Factor 3 :					
Promotional avenues			**0.861**		0.819
Scope for future growth and development in life as an employee in TTD			**0.765**		0.753
Authority and responsibility being enjoyed on the job			**0.650**		0.746
The present position in TTD			**0.573**		0.656
Transfer policy			**0.572**		0.574

169

Factor 4 :					
Working relationships among the colleagues				**0.786**	0.689
Nature of job currently doing				**0.634**	0.569
Being an employee in TTD				**0.620**	0.664
Superior-subordinate relationship				**0.598**	0.613
Eigen Value	8.479	2.329	1.707	1.455	
Variance (%)	42.393	11.645	8.536	85.8	
Cumulative variance (%)	42.393	54.039	62.574	69.849	
Reliability Alpha (%)	92.3	83.5	85.8	73.4	
Number of items (Total = 20)	6	5	5	4	

Note   : Extraction Method – Principal Component Analysis
Rotation Method – Varimax with Kaiser Normalization
KMO (Kaiser-Meyer-Olkim Measure of Sampling Adequacy) = 0.778
Bartlett's Test of Sphericity: $\underline{p}$ = 0.000 (x^2 = 5873.556, DF = 192
Sig =0.000*)

5.26 Correlation Analysis

A correlation coefficient measured the strength of a linear relationship between two variables. In the study, a correlation coefficient measured the strength of a linear relationship between the overall satisfaction of the respondents and four factors. The correlation between overall satisfaction and four factors was positive and was significant at 0.01 level (2-tailed). For example, the correlation between overall satisfaction and Factor 1 was 0.220* *($\underline{p}$=0.000); the correlation between overall satisfaction and Factor 2 was 0.359** ($\underline{p}$=0.000); the correlation between overall satisfaction and Factor3 was0.605** ($\underline{p}$=0.000), and the correlation between overall satisfaction and Factor 4 was 0.213** (P=0.000) (Table 5.26). Therefore, the study indicated that the correlation between overall satisfaction and factor1, factor2, factor3, factor4.

Table 5.26
Correlation between Overall Satisfaction and Four Factors

(N = 360)

		Factor 1	Factor 2	Factor 3	Factor 4
Overall Satisfaction	Pearson Correlation	0.220**	0.359**	0.605**	0.213**
	Sig. (2-tailed)	0.000	0.000	0.000	0.000
	N	360	360	360	360

**Correlation is significant at 0.01 level (2-tailed) * P < 0.05

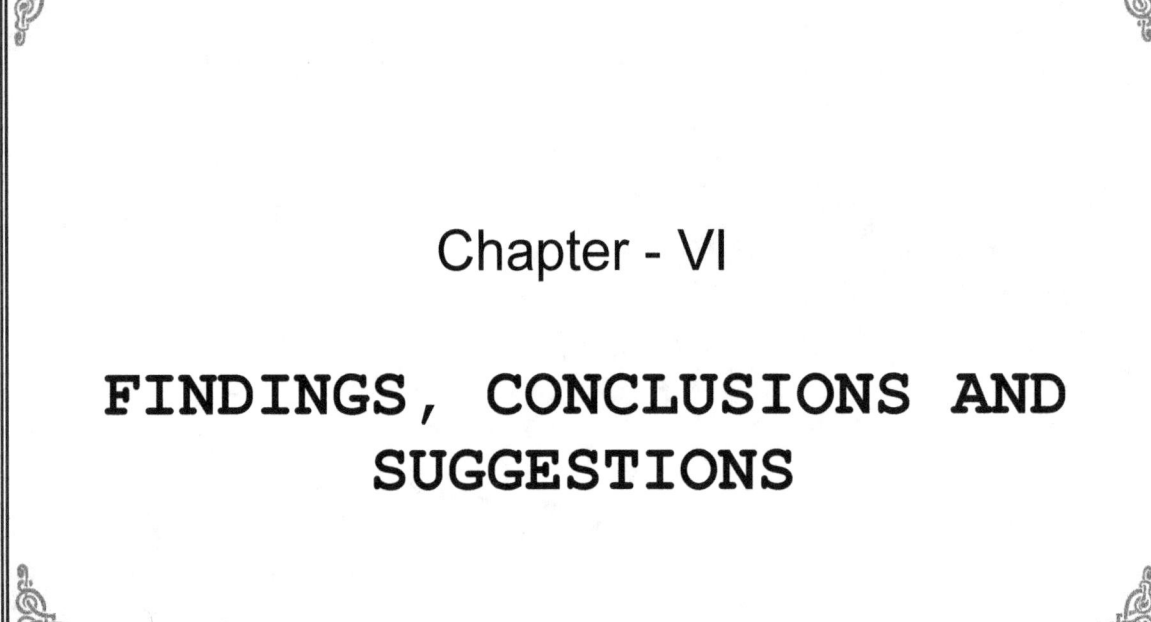

Chapter - VI

FINDINGS, CONCLUSIONS AND SUGGESTIONS

SUMMARY OF FINDINGS AND SUGGESTIONS

This chapter presents the summary of the findings of the study and offers suggestions to boost up the organizational climate and job satisfaction of the employees of the Tirumala Tirupati Davasthanams. It also proposes the scope for future research.

Organizational climate and job satisfaction play a significant role for an employee in terms of attitudes, beliefs and values, well-being and for an organization in terms of its productivity, efficiency, employee relations, absenteeism and turnover.

Job Satisfaction of TTD employees results from the specific likes and dislikes experienced in their jobs and TTD environment. The efficient manpower can be best utilized if employees are satisfied with their jobs. So, the ways in which authorities treat their employees and fulfil their needs and expectations can ensure the creation of a social environment conducive for harmonious employer-employee relationship.

For a detailed analysis and empirical evidence on organizational climate and job satisfaction, the employees of TTD, that is, the total sample universe for the study, comes to 360 employees. Of these, 36 are professionals, 109 are administrative staff and 215 are sub staff. Their responses to the structured questionnaire along with the published literature on the subject are the basis for arriving at meaningful conclusions of the study.

The data for the current study are pooled both from primary and secondary sources. Secondary data sources include electronic sources, published official reports on TTD, and published books, research articles, magazines, professional journals and daily newspapers, administrative Office and other places such as the Hindu religious and charitable endowments, Internet, theses and dissertations etc. However, primary data were generated canvassing the structured, pre-tested questionnaire to the sample respondents, for eliciting information on organizational climate and job satisfaction.

As such the entire questionnaire comprises three sections from 'A' to 'C'. Section 'A' incorporates questions designed to collect data on demographics of sample respondents, Section 'B' is related to organization climate variables, and

Section 'C' is focused on Job Satisfaction and requests the respondents to express their opinions on a five-point scale.

The collected data on organizational climate and job satisfaction are analyzed with the help of SPSS, statistical techniques like z-test, F- test, Chi – square test, correlation analysis, factor analysis and so on .They have been extensively used for testing the validity of the findings. The major findings of the study are presented as under.

6.1 SOCIO DEMOGRAPHIC VARIABLES OF THE RESPONDENTS

6.1.1 Designation of the Respondents

It is found from the study that the sample consists of 36 professionals, 109 administrative staff, and 215 sub staff. On the whole, 59.7 per cent of the respondents are the sub staff and the remaining 30.3 per cent are the administrative staff, 10 per cent are the professionals and their responses to the structured questionnaire are the basis for overall analysis and influences of the study (table 4.1).

6.1.2 Sex-wise Distribution

It is observed from the study that 68.3 per cent of the respondents in the sample are male and the rest are female. Further, the female employees according to category are also found to be very few (table 4.2).

6.1.3 Age- wise Distribution

It is observed from the study that a majority of respondents (37.2 per cent) belong to the age group of 36-40, while 32.8 per cent respondents are in the age group of 41-45, 18.9 per cent respondents are in the age group of 31-35, and 5.8 per cent respondents are in the age group of 46 and above. Around 5.3 per cent respondents belong to the age group of below 30 years (table 4.3).

6.1.4 Marital Status - wise Distribution

It is found from the study that 86.7 per cent of the respondents, on the whole, are married while 13.3 per cent are unmarried. Among the total unmarried respondents, professional respondents, administrative staff and sub staff respondents are 22.2 per cent, 17.4 per cent and 9.8 per cent. The chi-square value is significant at

5 per cent level, and it can be inferred that there is a significant difference between professionals, administrative staff, and sub staff with respect to marital status (table 4.4).

6.1.5 Social Status - wise distribution

It is noticed that, 36.4 per cent of respondents belong to other caste community, 32.8 per cent are from backward classes, 19.2 per cent belong to scheduled caste and 11.7 per cent of respondents are from scheduled tribe community. Category- wise distribution of sample respondents also indicates a similar trend. The chi-square value is significant at 5 per cent level and it can be inferred that there is a significant difference between professionals, administrative staff, and sub staff with respect to social status (table 4.5).

6.1.6 Family Size - wise Distribution

It is observed from the study that most of respondents are in the family size of four (39.2 per cent). About 23.6 per cent of the respondents have 3 members in their families, 18.1 per cent have 5 members in their families and 14.7 per cent have above 5 members. From this, one can deduce that the respondents in the present study prefer to have smaller families (table 4.6).

6.1.7 Family Background

It is also observed from the study that around 36.7 per cent of the employees selected for the study have an agriculture background. Similarly, 24.4 per cent respondents are from service families, 24.2 per cent of the employees are from others and 14.7 per cent of employees have come from business families (table 4.7).

6.1.8 Type of Family

It can be noticed that majority of the respondents (53.6 per cent) belong to nuclear families. This is because now-a-days people prefer to live independently than in a joint family set up. The remaining 46.4 per cent are from joint families. In this regard there is not much difference between professionals, administrative staff and sub staff respondents (table 4.8).

6.1.9 Total Earning Members in the Family

It is found that a majority of the respondents (61.9 per cent) i.e., 16 professional respondents, 69 administrative staff respondents and 138 sub staff respondents, have only one earning member in the family. Respondents belonging to families with two earning members constitute 26.4 per cent, 9 professional, 29 administrative staff, and 57 sub staff families, have three earning members and constitute 10.6 per cent (table 4.9).

6.1.10 Total Family Annual Income

It is clear that 52 respondents (14.4 per cent) earn below Rs. 1.5 lakhs, 184 respondents (15.1 per cent) earn between Rs. 1.5-2.0 lakhs, 83 respondents earn between Rs. 2.0-2.5 lakhs and 41 respondents earn Rs. 2.5 lakhs and above. The figures also reveal that category-wise, respondent's earning capacity is not similar, i.e., professional respondents (58.3 per cent) earn 2.50 lakhs and above, administrative staff respondents (65.1 per cent) earn between 1.50- 2.0 lakhs and sub staff respondents (50.7 per cent) earn between 1.50-2.0 lakhs (table 4.10).

6.1.11 Educational Qualifications

Most of the respondents have not even studied up to tenth standard. About 23 respondents have intermediate qualification, 88 respondents are graduates, 60 respondents post graduates, and a few respondents, i.e. 6.9 per cent, have professional degrees (table 4.11).

6.1.12 Technical Qualifications

It can be found from the table that 277 respondents (77 per cent) have no technical qualification, very few employees, i.e., 9 per cent, know typing, 8 per cent have PGDCA, 4 per cent DCA, and 1.4 per cent have B.Tech qualification (table 4.12).

6.1.13 Monthly Salary

About 40 per cent of the respondents are in the monthly salary range of 10,001-15,000, followed by 33.6 per cent respondents in the monthly salary range of Rs. 15,001-20,000, 18.1 per cent respondents in the monthly salary range of below

10,000 and 8 per cent of respondents in the monthly salary range of above 20,001 (table 4.13).

6.1.14 No. of Years of Service

It is noticed that 23.9 per cent of respondents have between 16-20 years service. The data also reveals that the respondents who have put in 11-15 years of service account for 27.8 per cent, respondents with less than 5 years service constitute 13.3 per cent and those with 6-10 years of service are 11.1 per cent (table 4.14).

6.1.15 No. of Promotions

On the whole, most of the sample employees (73.3 per cent) had no promotion. Further, 19 per cent of respondents have been promoted once, and 6.9 per cent of respondents have received promotion twice (table 4.15).

6.1.16 No. of Awards and Rewards

It is observed from the study that with regard to the details of awards and rewards either in the form of monetary rewards or in the form of letter of appreciation by the respondents, a majority (98 per cent) of the respondents did not receive any kind of awards and rewards in their career. Very few respondents have received monetary awards and rewards (1.1 per cent). Only 6 per cent of respondents have received non-monetary awards and rewards (Table 4.16).

6.1.17 No.of Employee Training Programmes

It is witnessed that except for 145 respondents (40 per cent), all the respondents have attended the training programmes. Further, it is observed that about 22.2 per cent of respondents comprising professionals 3, administrative staff 16, and sub staff 61 respondents attended training programmes once. Among those who attended four times or more, professionals are 13.9 per cent, administrative staff are 22 per cent and sub staff respondents are 20 per cent respectively (table 4.17).

MEASUREMENT OF ORGANIZATIONAL CLIMATE

6.1.18 Managerial structure and policies:

It is found that the respondents moderately accept 'The policies and goals of the T.T.D are clearly understood' (3.49). Similarly those who agree with in TTD the formal authority takes decisions are (3.39), those who agree with the job in TTD is clearly defined and structured logically are (3.39) and those who agree with the TTD recruits people after objective assessment of the merits of each case are (3.33). 'Information relating to job or policy is communicated to employee through established channels are' (2.96) and 'Service rules and policies are consistently followed in TTD while dealing with the employee's personal matters' are (3.08) (table 4.18) respectively. The mean scores of those who agree with statements are given in brackets.

Therefore, it can be said that management can influence organizational climate by changing policies, rules and procedure .This may take time, but the change is long lasting if the employees see the change in policies as favourable to them.

6.1.19 Recognition and Appreciation

It is noticed in the present study that the respondents well agreed with the statements 'I feel that I am a valuable member of a team working in TTD' (3.74), 'in TTD, the management always recognizes good work' (3.58) and 'there is recognition for merit, talent and qualifications in TTD' (3.41) shows that the working team is on the higher side. There is a weak agreement (2.85) with the view 'suggestions given by me for improvement are well appreciated and recognized by superior' and (2.85) 'the work of mine is done by colleagues' better manner he/she will get proper recognition'(3.10). So, it can be said that the recognition and appreciation is fairly common in TTD organization (table 4.19).

6.1.20 Participative Management

The respondents have indicated some agreement with the view that management is participative. The view- 'before taking any important decision, the management of TTD always consults the employees' (2.89) is less acceptable and the statements 'The management gives due respect and power to the workers representatives in meetings' (3.3 1) is moderately agreeable. The view' the representatives of various committees in TTD are capable and competent (3.13)' is less agreeable. The TTD organization gives due respect to workers' representatives, but there is less participative management in TTD organization (table 4.20).

6.1.21 Supervision

It is observed from the study that they are close to agreement with the statements, 'The main purpose of supervision is to ensure achievement of targets' (3.63) followed by 'Superiors in our organization expect subordinates to do the job strictly according to rules' (3.53), 'Supervision in our organization helps to maintain good relations with subordinate' (3.47) and 'My superiors give help and support' (3.40). There is moderate agreement with the views, 'Superiors in our organization usually check mistakes and punish subordinates' (3.19) and 'My superior listens to what I have to say' (3.02). From this, it can be concluded that supervision is perceived as fair in TTD organization (table 4.21).

6.1.22 Conflict Avoidance

It is noticed that the respondents have shown agreement with the statements that indicate- "Conflicts are usually avoided and people prefer friendly atmosphere in TTD' (3.68), and 'Experts are consulted and their advice is sought in resolving conflicts' (3.45). The perception shows that conflict avoidance system is well organised in TTD organization (table 4.22).

6.1.23 Warmth

It is evident that the respondents perceive this dimension positively. They agree that, 'A Friendly atmosphere prevails among the employees in TTD' (3.71). They also perceive 'There is a lot of warmth in the relationship between management and employees in TTD' (3.39) and 'In TTD there is a relaxed and easy going working climate' (3.25). In view of this, it can be said that the warmth is reasonably good (table 4.23).

6.1.24 Social Values

It is noticed in the present study that the respondents have agreed well with the statements." I am proud to be a member of TTD (4.08). They have also agreed with the statements that 'I have high satisfaction that I am rendering social service to the society through TTD' (4.01), 'The management of TTD encourages us to take part in social service and cultural programmes' (3.91) and also 'TTD organization gives special attention to fulfill the social needs of the employees, in order to increase their social values' (3.49). The findings indicate that employees are proud to be members in this organization and Social Values in TTD organization are protected very well (table 4.24).

6.1.25 Training and Advancement

It is observed from the respondent's views that there are 'adequate training programmes and facilities' (3.71). Around (3.48) agreed with 'I have had sufficient job related training' (3.33) agreed with 'TTD plans on regular basis for ensuring its employees career development' and (3.29) with 'opportunities for their career advancement' are available in TTD organization. Therefore, it can be said that the dimension- Training and Advancement- is perceived as fair in TTD organization. But with regard to change in training and advancement, there should be ample scope for growth of each person in an organization and organization must strive for overall development of staff. New CEO brings such changes after joining the TTD organization (Table 4.25).

6.1.26 Grievance Handling

The three statements 'The TTD is always ready to handle the grievances and complaints of the employees' (3.14) 'The grievance handling and settlement system existing in the TTD is effective' (3.03) and I am satisfied with the present system of grievance handling procedure in TTD (3.04), are moderately acceptable to the respondents. Therefore, it can be stated that grievance handling is above average and requires further improvement (table 4.26).

6.1.27 Individual Autonomy

It is evident from the perception on individual autonomy that the respondents have shown themselves to be undecided with the statements that indicate 'Employees are free to set their own performance goals' (3.09) and 'work gives me opportunity of freedom and independence' (3.00). This is indicative of Individual Autonomy the TTD employees have at work place (table 4.27).

6.1.28 Individual Responsibility

It is observed from the study that the respondents have agreed well with the statements – 'I always feel responsible at work' (3.76) and 'If at times things do not go well, I do take responsibility' (3.74). From this, it can be concluded that individual responsibility is perceived well by the respondents (table 4.28).

6.1.29 Performance Standards

It is evident from the study that the respondents have shown moderate agreement with the statements – 'In TTD importance is given for high quality of work' (3.30) as well as 'The problems that are relating to work are solved quickly' (3.30) It follows, 'The goals that are set by the TTD are communicated to all the members to achieve them' (3.26) 'In TTD we set very high Standards for performance' (3.25) and 'There are rules and regulations for handling any kind of problem, which may arise in making most of the decisions'(2.97). From this, it can be understood that reasonable standards are maintained for better performance and it needs further improvement (table 4.29).

6.1.30 Mutual Trust

It is found from the study that the respondents are well agreed with the statements that indicate- 'Employees in this organization really trust each other very much' (3.52), 'There is high trust between superiors and subordinates in the TTD organization' (3.38) as well as 'Specialists and experts are highly trusted in TTD' (3.38)'and 'Those who can achieve good results in the TTD organization are highly trusted' (3.19). From this, it can be understood that there is a reasonable level of mutual trust (table 4.30).

6.1.31 Awards and rewards system

With regard to awards and rewards system, the respondents are neutral to the statements. 'Employees who keep up the tradition in this organization are duly recognized and rewarded' (3.22). 'The management of TTD recognizes the efficiency of one's own work and accordingly employees are awarded' (3.12)'Team work in the TTD organization is encouraged and rewarded' (3.08), 'Anything goes wrong with the employees, such employees are seriously reprimanded or punished'(3.05)and 'Excellence in performance and getting tasks accomplished are highly rewarded in the TTD organization (2.85) (table 4.31).

6.1.32 Work Relation

The relations among the colleagues in our organization are healthy and friendly' (3.77) 'Employees in TTD are very much concerned to help each other spontaneously when ever need arises' (3.61) and 'The working relations between superiors and subordinates in TTD are so cordial' (3.45).). From this, it can be concluded that Work Relations in TTD are perceived well by the respondents (table 4.32).

6.1.33 Decision Making

With regard to decision making the respondents disagree with the statements that indicate –'decisions are made in consultation with the unions in TTD' (2.79), mainly the experts are involved in the decision making process' (2.76)', and how often are you involved in decision making' (2.14). The findings indicate that employees are not involved in decision-making process. The employees should be involved in goal setting and taking decisions that influence their lot. They will feel committed to the organization and exhibit an attitude of co-operation (table 4.33).

6.1.34 Welfare Facilities

The respondents have agreed well with the statements, 'Medical facilities/ medical reimbursement provided by the employer are adequate' (3.84). It is followed by 'The Management of TTD provides adequate and qualitative educational services to the children of employees' (3.63), 'TTD administration provides housing accommodation with water facilities at reasonable cost' (3.48), 'I am satisfied with the transport facilities from home to the work place' (3.47), 'TTD provides attractive retirement benefits to its employees' (3.58) and ' The welfare facilities provided by TTD are far better than the welfare facilities provided by Govt'(3.44). From this, it can be concluded that welfare facilities are perceived very well by respondents in TTD organization (table 4.34).

6.1.35 Communication

With agreed to perceptions of respondents on communication, there is moderate agreements with the statements such as 'One way communication that is from top to bottom is in vogue in TTD' (3.30), 'Upward communication is accurate in our organization' (3.18), 'There is good communication across all sections in' (3.11) 'Relevant information is available to all those who need and can use such information' (3.14), 'Employees are taking initiative in communicating concern for others' (3.03) and 'Communication between subordinates and superiors is always open' (3.13) (table 4.35).

6.1.36 Unions

With regard to unions the respondents perceive this dimension with moderate agreement expressing   views such as -'TTD is not opposing the formation and functioning of the unions' (3.32) as well as 'Trade union leadership is acquired on democratic lines in our organization' (3.18). It followed by views like 'Issues for collective bargaining are determined with the consultation of union members', (3.17) 'Unions in my organization are effective in solving their problems of the employees' (3.11), 'There is no inter-union rivalry in this organization'(3.06) and 'Union-management relations are cordial'(3.01). As such, it can be said that the dimension of union is perceived as positive in TTD organization (table 4.36).

6.1.37 Organisational Climate and Personal Variables

With reference to each of the personal variables i.e, gender, age, income, education and experience, dimension wise analysis of perception of respondents' employees on organizational climate is presented in table 4.38 to 4.44. To find out if there are significant differences of   organizational climate across each variable, the respondents are analyzed using z-test. Under each group, means and standard deviations are calculated for each dimension of OC. F-value for large sample means was performed for each organizational climate dimension.

6.1.38 Perception Across Gender

The results of z-test on means for each dimension across gender are furnished in (table 4.38). Therefore, it can be concluded that gender has no influence on the perceptions of the organizational climate. Therefore, the hypothesis formulated that there is no significant difference between gender and organizational climate is accepted

6.1.39 Perceptions Across Age

The results of F-test for each dimension across the three age groups viz., lower age (< 30 years), middle age (30 years to 35 years) and higher age (35 years and above) are furnished in (table 4.39). Under each age group, means and standard deviations are calculated for each dimension of organizational climate and F-values are performed to detect statistically significant differences across age group. Statistically significant difference across age group has been found for 6 out of 19 dimensions of organizational climate. These are: Managerial Structure and policies, supervision, social Values, awards and rewards system, work relation, and welfare Facilities.

Therefore, lower age group (< 30 years) influences the perceptions of the organizational climate. Therefore, the hypothesis formulated that there is significant difference between age and organizational climate is rejected.

6.1.40 Perceptions Across   Monthly Salary

With regard to monthly salary that there is significant difference in the perception on organizational climate across the income levels of respondents, the perceptions are tabulated across different income groups. Income groups are classified into lower income (up to Rs. 10,000), middle income (Rs. 10,001 to Rs. 20,000) and higher income (more than Rs. 20,000) groups. Under each income group, means and standard deviations were calculated for each dimension of organizational climate. F-test is done for each organizational climate dimension across income to know the statistically significant differences. Statistically significant differences are found in respect of 11 out of 19 items (table 4. 40). They are:

Managerial Structure and policies; Recognition and appreciation; Supervision; Conflict avoidance; Social Values; Individual Responsibility; Performance Standards; Mutual Trust; Awards and rewards system; decision-making; and welfare facilities; Therefore, it can be said that monthly salary of higher level income (more than Rs. 20,000) groups has greater influence on the perception on organizational climate. So, the hypothesis formulated that there is significant difference between monthly salary and organizational climate is rejected.

6.1.41 Perceptions Across Education

On the basis of educational level, respondents were divided into three groups viz., highly educated (post graduate and above), moderately educated (graduates) and low those with level of education (intermediate and below) (table 4.41). F-test is done for each organizational climate dimension across education to know the statistically significant differences. Statistically significant differences are found in respect of 13 out of 19 items. They are:

Managerial Structure and policies; Recognition and appreciation; Supervision; Conflict avoidance; Social Values; Training and advancement; Grievance Handling; Individual Autonomy; Performance Standards; Mutual Trust; Awards and rewards system; decision-making; and welfare facilities;

The results indicate that higher education has shown greater influence on the perception on organizational climate dimension. So, the hypothesis formulated that there exists significant difference between education and organizational climate is rejected.

6.1.42 Perceptions Across Experience

It is observed from the study that experience influences the perceptions of respondents. Based on length of service, three groups are formed: low (up to 10 years), medium (10 years to 15 years) and high (more than 16 years) groups were classified. F-test is done for each organizational climate dimension across experience to know the statistically significant differences. Statistically significant differences are found in respect of 12 out of 19 items (table 4.42). They are:

185

Managerial Structure and policies; Recognition and appreciation; Conflict avoidance; warmth; Social Values; Grievance Handling; Individual Responsibility; Awards and rewards system; work relation; decision-making; welfare facilities; and communication

The results indicate that low (up to 10 years) service group has shown greater influence on the perception on organizational climate dimension. Therefore, the hypothesis formulated that there is significant difference between service and organizational climate is rejected

6.1.43 Perceptions Across Designation

F-test is done for each organizational climate dimension across designation to know the statistically significant differences. Statistically significant differences are found in respect of 18 out of 19 items. The results indicate that professionals group has shown greater influence on the perception on organizational climate dimensions. So, the hypothesis formulated that there exists significant difference between designation and organizational climate is rejected (table 4.44).

6.1.44 Correlation Analysis

Correlation between OC and demographic variables is presented in table 4.43.To further examine the validity of the hypothesis, correlations between the personal variables such as age, gender, income, education and experience and perceptions of respondent employees on organizational climate scores are found. Table 4.43 shows a lack of association of the perceptions with age, gender, income, education and experience variables has significant correlation at 0.01level with about 12 of the dimensions and also with overall climate. However, the coefficients are negative and below 0.05 indicating a weak negative relationship

6.2. Measurement of Job satisfaction

Job Satisfaction has been regarded both as a general attitude as well as satisfaction with specific dimensions of the job such as salary, the work itself, promotional opportunities, supervision, coworkers and so forth. These may interact in different ways to create the feeling of satisfaction with the job. The degree of satisfaction may vary with how well outcomes fulfill or exceed expectations. Therefore, job satisfaction is acknowledged as the most well known, frequently measured and extensively researched work attitude especially in the areas of organizational behaviour and human resource management. For comprehensive analysis, the level of job satisfaction is measured on 20 dimensions. The scale of measurement of job satisfaction is based on five point Likert's method of summated ratings which has the practical advantage of simplicity and ease of construction and, at the same time, does not violate any important theoretical considerations. Each dimension has five alternative responses from satisfied to highly dissatisfied. The result of overall job satisfaction with personal variables is discussed below.

6.2.1   Designation and Job Satisfaction

It is evident from table 5.1 that the majority of respondents (45.45 per cent) or administrative staff are in the high satisfaction category. The respondents who are professionals (10.99 per cent), sub staff (59.22 per cent), and administrative staff (29.79 per cent) are in the moderate satisfaction category, whereas the majority of respondents (85.29 per cent) belonging to sub staff fall in the low satisfaction category. The chi-square value is given by 15.603 which is highly significant at 1 per cent level. It reveals that there is significant association between designation and job satisfaction. The null hypothesis formulated for job satisfaction is rejected.

6.2.2   Sex and job Satisfaction

Table 5.2 presents sex-wise job satisfaction among the selected respondents. It is found that of the majority of the respondents, 86.36 per cent, 62.41 per cent, and 94.12 per cent of male employees belong to high, moderate, and low satisfaction levels respectively when compared to female respondents.

There is a general feeling that there exists an association between sex and job satisfaction. It is proved in the present study. The chi-square value is given by 21.627which is highly significant at 1 per cent level. It reveals that there is significant

187

association between sex and job satisfaction. The null hypothesis formulated for job satisfaction is rejected.

6.2.3 Age and Job Satisfaction

Age is supposed to have some relation to job satisfaction. However, when the data were categorized according to high, medium and low satisfaction groups, five age categories (table 5.3) are tested for association. The chi-square value is given by 37.749which is highly significant at 1 per cent level. It reveals that there is significant association between age and job satisfaction. However, 40.91 per cent of respondents in the age group 36-40 are in high satisfaction level. The majority of the respondents (5.67 per cent) are in the age group below 30, 19.15 per cent of respondents are in the age group between 31-35, and 32.62 per cent of respondents are in age group between 41 -45 and belong to moderate satisfaction levels. Majority of the respondents are in the age group 46 and above and 26.47 per cent fall in the low satisfaction level. The null hypothesis formulated for job satisfaction is rejected.

6.2.4 Marital Status and Job Satisfaction

It is clear from table 5.4 that the majority of the respondents (79.55 per cent, 86.52per cent, and 97.06per cent) are married employees who belong to satisfaction levels, high, medium, and low respectively. Some studies indicated that married employees have some added responsibilities as compared to unmarried employees. As a result, married employees have better adjustment to their work situation and hence, higher job satisfaction than unmarried employees. These indicate that marital status has no impact on level of satisfaction. Chi-square values computed also are found to be not significant in marital status. Thus, it can be concluded that there is no significant relationship between marital status and job satisfaction. The null hypothesis is accepted.

6.2.5 Social Status and Job Satisfaction

Table 5.5 reveals the details of social status and job satisfaction. It is noticed from the table that the majority of (50 per cent) respondents in OC category have high job satisfaction, whereas, 25 per cent of respondents in BC, 11.36 per cent of respondents in SC, and 13.64 per cent of respondents in ST category have high satisfaction levels. The chi-square value is given by 12.995which is significant at 5 per cent level. It reveals that there is significant association between social status and job satisfaction. The null hypothesis formulated for job satisfaction is rejected.

6.2.6 Family Size and Job Satisfaction

Employees having smaller families (having less number of dependents) will be relatively more satisfied than those having larger families. It is noticed that table 5.6 reveals the relationship between family size and job satisfaction. 29.55 per cent of respondents belonging to families with 3 or 4 members are in high satisfaction groups, whereas, 42.20 per cent of respondents belonging to family size of four fall in medium satisfaction category and 29.41 per cent of respondents belonging to family size three are in the low satisfaction category. Chi- square value is not significant. From this, it can be understood that there is no association between family size and job satisfaction. So, the null hypothesis is accepted.

6.2.7 Family Background and Job Satisfaction

Family background of the employees and details of their level of job satisfaction details are presented in table 5.7. It is observed that the majority (36.36 per cent) of respondents with agriculture as family background have high satisfaction, whereas 35.82 per cent, 44.12 per cent of respondents with an agriculture family background belong to moderate and low satisfaction groups respectively. 17.38 per cent of respondents with a business family background have perceived moderate satisfaction, whereas, 9.09 per cent fall in the high satisfaction category. 25 per cent of respondents have service as family back ground and have high satisfaction, whereas, 35.29 per cent of respondents have low satisfaction. With regard to other family back ground 29.55 per cent have high satisfaction, whereas 20.59 per cent have low satisfaction. The chi-square value is not significant. There is no relationship between family background and job satisfaction. So, the null hypothesis is accepted.

6.2.8 Type of Family and Job Satisfaction

Type of family (joint/ nuclear) may be an important factor of job satisfaction. Table 5.8 shows distribution of respondents according to type of family and level of job satisfaction. It can be noticed from table 5.8 that the majority of respondents (54.55 per cent) belong to joint family type and 45.45 per cent of respondents to nuclear type of family. They are in high satisfaction category. 58.16 per cent of respondents belonging to nuclear family type fall in moderate satisfaction category, and 73.53 per cent of respondents of belonging to joint family type fall in the low satisfaction. The chi-square value is given by 13.590which is highly significant at 1 per cent level. It reveals that there is significant association between type of family and job satisfaction. The null hypothesis formulated for job satisfaction is rejected.

6.2.9   Total Earning Members in the Family and Job satisfaction

It can be seen from table 5.9 that the employees are classified in to high (59.09 per cent), moderate (59.22 per cent) and low (88.24 per cent) job satisfaction groups with one earning member in the family, 29.08 per cent of the respondents are perceived to be in the moderate satisfaction group, 20.45 per cent of respondents have high job satisfaction, and 11.76 per cent of the respondents with two earning members in the family have low satisfaction. 18.18 per cent of respondents have high job satisfaction and have three earning members in the family, whereas 2.27 per cent of respondents have high satisfaction groups and have four and above earning members in the family. Therefore, it can be confirmed that there exists no relationship between total earning members in the family and job satisfaction. Chi-square value is not significant. Hence, the null hypothesis is accepted.

6.2.10 Total Family Annual Income and Job Satisfaction

Income is also a significant factor of job satisfaction. If the employees feel that income they get is commensurate with their contribution, they will be satisfied. Thus there is positive relationship between total family annual income and job satisfaction. Table 5.10 shows distribution of sample employees according to income and job satisfaction.

It can be observed from table 5.10, that majority (56.82 per cent) of the respondents with annual income between Rs.1.5 2.0 lakhs have high job satisfaction 46.81 per cent of respondents with income between Rs. 1.5-2.0 lakhs, 14.89 per cent of respondents have income below 1.5 lakhs, 26.24 per cent of respondents with income between 2 – 2.5 lakhs fall in moderate satisfaction group and majority (79.41 per cent) of the respondents, irrespective of their income levels, belong to low satisfaction group. The chi-square value is given by 17.551 which is highly significant at 1 per cent level. It reveals that there is significant association between total family annual income and job satisfaction. The null hypothesis formulated for job satisfaction is rejected.

6.2.11 Educational Qualification and Job Satisfaction

Table 5.11 gives the details of relationship between educational qualification and job satisfaction. Of the majority of the respondents, 31.82 per cent of employees belong to graduates,11.36 per cent of respondents belong to professional courses and 25 per cent of respondents belong to P.G and those with below 10th qualification have high level of satisfaction, whereas 45.39 per cent respondents, with below 10th class education qualification, fall in moderate satisfaction group. The chi-square value is given by 23.135 which is highly significant at 1 per cent level. It reveals that there is significant association between educational qualification and job satisfaction. The null hypothesis formulated for job satisfaction is rejected.

6.2.12 Technical Qualification and Job Satisfaction

Table 5.12 shows the relationship between technical qualification and job satisfaction. Most of the respondents with no technical qualification belong satisfaction levels high, moderate and low. The chi-square value is given by 16.354which is significant at 5 per cent level. It reveals that there is significant association between technical qualification and job satisfaction. The null hypothesis formulated for job satisfaction is rejected.

6.2.13 Monthly Salary and Job Satisfaction

Details of monthly salary and job satisfaction are presented in table 5.13. It can be noted from the table that majority (47.73 per cent) of the respondents with monthly income between Rs. 10,000 – 15, 000, (22.73 per cent) of respondents with monthly income below 10,000are in high satisfaction groups, majority (10.28 per cent) of respondents with monthly income above 20,000 fall in the moderate satisfaction group, and 50 per cent of respondents with monthly income between Rs. 15,000 – 20,000 fall in the low satisfaction group. The chi- square value is not significant. So, it implies that there is no association between monthly salary and job satisfaction; hence, the null hypothesis is accepted.

6.2.14 No. Of Years of Service and Job Satisfaction

Several investigations have revealed that there is a positive relationship between number of years service and job satisfaction. Employees with greater experience tend to be more satisfied with their jobs. This is because of their better adjustment to work situation stemming from experience with it. The length of service in the organization broadens the knowledge of the employees about the organization and develops a sort of loyalty and attachment to the concern. Table 5.14 shows relationship between number of years of service and job satisfaction.

It is observed from table 5.14 that the majority (25 per cent) of respondents having number of years service ranging from 16 – 20 years have high satisfaction, whereas employees (30.14 per cent) having service ranging from 11- 15 years have moderate satisfaction and majority (61.76 per cent) of respondents having service ranging from 20 years and above fall in the low satisfaction category. The chi-square value is given by 38.206 which is highly significant at 1 per cent level. It reveals that there is significant association between number of years service and job satisfaction. The null hypothesis formulated for job satisfaction is rejected.

6.2.15 Promotions and Job Satisfaction

Promotion is an advancement of an employee to a better job, better in terms of greater responsibilities, more prestige, and greater skills. Hence it significantly affects job satisfaction. Table 5.15 shows relationship between numbers of promotions received so far and job satisfaction. It is observed from the table 5.15 that the 27 respondents who have not received any promotions (61.36 per cent) are in high satisfaction group, whereas, most of the respondents (73.40 per cent, and 88.24 per cent) who have not received any promotions fall in moderate and low satisfaction groups. Chi-square values computed in this regard are found to be not significant. There is no significant relationship between number of promotions received and job satisfaction. Hence, the null hypothesis is accepted.

6.2.16 Awards and Rewards and Job Satisfaction

From table 5.16, it is clear that there is a definite relation between job satisfaction and awards and rewards received by the employees. However, more than 98 per cent of the respondents have not received any kind of award and rewards in TTD. The chi-square value is not significant. It can be concluded that there is no relationship between number of awards and rewards received and job Satisfaction. The hypothesis so formulated is accepted.

6.2.17 Training Programmes attended and Job satisfaction

Table 5.17 witnessed an association between training programmes attended and the felt job satisfaction. Majority (29.55 per cent) of the respondents who attended training programmes once belong to those with high level of satisfaction. 48.94 per cent of the respondents who did not attend training programmes fall in moderate satisfaction category, whereas, 47.06 per cent of the respondents who attended training programmes once fall in the low satisfaction category. The chi-square value is given by 57.699 which is highly significant at 1 per cent level. It reveals that there is significant association between training programmes and job satisfaction. The null hypothesis formulated for job satisfaction is rejected.

6.2.18 Aspects of Job satisfaction

Table 5.18 reveals that the mean score values are in the range of 2.65 and 4.06 indicating that most of the respondents are satisfied with their jobs. In fact, six factors viz., Administrative policies of the TTD, Superior-Subordinate relationship, Authority and responsibility being enjoyed on the job, Scope for future growth and development in life as an employee in TTD, Transfer Policy, and Promotional Avenues are dissatisfaction factors. The researcher assumed that mean score below 3.50 are dissatisfaction aspects.

6.2.19 Factor Analysis for Job satisfaction

Table 5.25 shows the result of Factor analysis by principal components analysis method which is applied on 20 variables of job satisfaction. The researcher reduced them into four major factors, namely, Factor 1, factor 2, factor 3, and factor 4.

Factor 1 contained six attributes and explained 42.393 % of the variance in the data, with an eigen value of 8.479 and a reliability of 92.3 %.

Factor 2 accounted for 11.64 % of the variance, with an eigen value of 2.329 and a reliability of 83.5 %. This factor was loaded with 5 attributes

Factor 3 is loaded with five attributes. This factor accounted for 8.536 % of the variance, with an eigen value of 1.707 and a reliability of 85.8 %.

Factor 4 contained four attributes that referred to job satisfaction aspects. This factor explained 85.8 % of the variance, with an eigen value of 1.455 and a reliability of 73.4.

CONCLUSIONS

Most of the respondents (61.9 per cent) have one earning member in the family. On the whole, 76.9 per cent of the respondents have no technical qualification. Most of the respondents have not received promotions so far in TTD (73.3 per cent). As far as number of years of service is concerned, those with 11-15 service are 27.8 per cent, 16-20 years service 23.9 per cent, and those who have 20 years above service are 23.9 per cent. On the whole, 98.3 per cent of the respondents have not received any awards and rewards.

Majority of the respondents, are agreed upon dimensions like welfare facilities, work relation, individual responsibility, social values and conflict avoidance. They are less agreed upon the dimensions of decision making, grievance handling, individual autonomy and participative management. The respondents are moderately agreed upon the dimensions of Performance standards, mutual trust, recognition and appreciation.

Majority of the respondents are highly satisfied being employees of TTD with regard to promotional avenues, transfer policy, scope for future growth and development in life. Regarding authority and responsibility and enjoying the job, there is a negative opinion and dissatisfaction among the employees of TTD. In the case of employees of TTD, salary in relation to experience on the job and salary being drawn on the current job, salary in relation to educational qualification are factors that enhance job satisfaction.

Gender has no influence on the perception of the organizational climate. The younger age (below 30 years) influences the perceptions of the organizational climate when compared to middle age (30 years to 35 years) and higher age (35 years and above). The monthly salary of higher level income (income than Rs.20,000) groups has greater influence on the perception on organizational climate. The results indicate that higher education has shown greater influence on the perception on organizational climate. It is found that short length of (up to 10 years) service has shown greater influence on the perception on organizational climate.

195

Organizational climate is a manifestation of the attitudes of organizational members towards the organization. Organizational climate influences to a great extent the performance of the employees because it has a major impact on motivation and job satisfaction of individual employees. Organizational climate determines the work environment in which the employees feel satisfied or dissatisfied. Since satisfaction determines or influences the efficiency of the employees, the researcher can say that organizational climate is directly related to the efficiency and performance of the employees in TTD.

SUGGESTIONS

In the light of the findings arrived at in the study, the following suggestions are offered to ensure positive perception towards various variables of organizational climate which enhance job satisfaction among the employees of TTD.

Organizational climate factors such as awards and rewards system, individual autonomy, managerial structure and policies, performance of standards, recognition and appreciation, and unions have been moderately agreed upon by majority of the selected respondents. Hence, the TTD administration should take the initiative and appropriate measures to ensure a positive attitude towards the said factors. This, will, in the long run, give scope for enhancing positive attitude towards organisational climate that will lead to enhanced job satisfaction among the employees.

About 98 per cent of the respondents have not received any kind of award or rewards in TTD. So there is a need for maintaining and improving the awards and rewards systems to provide recognition and to make them proud of their performance. Communication and decision making have been less agreed upon by majority of the respondents. If decision making is decentralized and the incumbent is allowed to decentralize decision making it will enhance job satisfaction. To participate in decision making it is not needed to check each and every matter with the higher echelons. Therefore, TTD administration should try to improve the above dimension.

It is noticed in the present study that the Administrative polices, superior – subordinate relations, authority and responsibility, scope for future growth and development, transfer policy and promotional avenues have been treated as dissatisfaction factors. Therefore, it is suggested that if employees' performance and job satisfaction are to be improved, the management must modify these factors. Hence, efforts are to be initiated to make job more interesting by safeguarding the personal life, ensuring retirement packages and formulating new guidelines for transfer policy.

It is observed that TTD organization gives due respect to workers' representatives but there is less participative management in TTD organization. So, employee participation is a very effective tool to develop sound participation based on democratic values of organizational life. There is a need to improve Participative Management in TTD.

Though the sub-staff in TTD are satisfied with their salary, in the case of promotions, the sub-staff are not satisfied. So, there is a need to improve the promotional facilities with regard to sub-staff in TTD.

Good organizational climate is instrumental in ensuring higher employee satisfaction, better human relations and higher productivity. The role of climate has thus a direct impact on human behaviour, their performance, satisfaction and attitude.

Questionnaire

STRUCTURED QUESTIONNAIRE ON
AN EMPIRICAL STUDY ON ORGANIZATIONAL CLIMATE AND JOB SATISFACTION IN TIRUMALA AND TIRUPATI DEVASTHANAM

Research Supervisor
Dr.M.Venkateswarlu
Associate Professor
Department of Commerce
Sri Venkateswara University
Tirupati – 517 502
Andhra Pradesh.

Research Scholar
C.Brahmaiah
Department of Commerce
S.V.University
Tirupati – 517 502
Cell: 95053 37510

(I)The information that you provide while filling this questionnaire will be kept confidential and used exclusively for research purpose. Therefore, I request you to give opinions freely and fairly.

(A) **Personal background of the employee**

1. Name of the employee _____

2. Designation

3. Sex : (1) Male (2) Female   [ ]

4. Age (in years)   [ ]

(1) Below 25 (2) 26 - 35 (3) 36 - 45 (4) 46 – 55 (5) 56 and above

5. Marital Status   [ ]

      (1) Married (2) Unmarried

6. Social Status   [ ]

      (1) OC (2) BC (3) SC (4) ST

7. Family Size (including children)   [ ]

      (1) 2 (2) 3 (3) 4 (4) 5 (5) Above 5

8. Family Background   [ ]

      (1) Agriculture (2) Business (3) Service (4) Others

9. Type of Family   [ ]

      (1) Joint family (2) Nuclear family

10. Total Earning Members in the family   [ ]

      (1) 1 (2) 2 (3) 3 (4) 4 and Above

11. Total family annual income (approximate)   [ ]

      (1) Below Rs.150000 (2) Rs.150001 - 200000

      (3) Rs. 200001 - 250000 (4) Rs.250000 and Above

12. Educational qualifications [ ]

        (1) S.S.C/SSLC (2) Inter / PUC (3) Degree (4) P.G (5) M.Phil (6) Ph.D

13. Technical qualifications [ ]

        (1) Typing (2) DCA (3) PGDCA (4) B.Tech (5) M.Tech

14. Monthly Salary [ ]

        (1) Below Rs.6000 (2) Rs.6001 - 10000

        (3) Rs. 10001 - 15000 (4) above Rs.15001-20000 (5) Above 20000

15. No. of years of service in T.T.D [ ]

        (1) Below 5 (2) 6-10 (3) 11 - 15 (4) 16-20 (5) 20 and Above

16. No. of promotions received so far in T.T.D [ ]

        (1) Nil (2) Once (3) Twice (4) Three times (5) Four times and above

17. No. of Awards and rewards received if any [ ]

        (1) Not received (2) Monetary (3) Non-monetary

18. No. of employee training programmes attended [ ]

        (1) Not attended (2) 1 (3) 2 (4) 3 (5) 4 and above

(II) Here under some aspects of **organizational climate** in the form of statements in T.T.D are given. You are requested to go through the following questions meticulously and select the appropriate response you feel right from among the given alternatives on a **FIVE POINT SCALE** as mentioned below. You are requested to read the statements.

5. SA - Strongly Agree

4. A - Agree

3. UN - Undecided

2. D - Disagree

1. SD - Strongly Disagree

Managerial structure and policies:

19. The policies and goals of the T.T.D are clearly understood [ ]

20. Service rules and policies are consistently followed in TTD while dealing with the employees personal matters [ ]

21. Information relating to job or policy is communicated to employee through established channels [ ]

22. The TTD recruits people after objective assessment of the merits of each case [ ]

200

23. In TTD the formal authority takes decisions [ ]

24. The job in TTD is clearly defined and structured logically [ ]

Recognition and Appreciation:

25. I feel that I am a valuable member of a team working in TTD [ ]

26. In TTD, the management always recognizes good work [ ]

27. There is recognition for merit, talent and qualifications in TTD [ ]

28. The work of mine is done by colleagues' better manner he/she will get [ ]
proper recognition

29. Suggestions given for me for improvement are well appreciated recognized [ ]
by superior

Participative Management:

30 The management gives due respect and power to the workers representatives [ ]
in meetings

31 Before taking any important decision, the management always in TTD always [ ]
consults the employees

32. The representatives of various committees in TTD are capable and competent [ ]

Supervision:

33 Supervision in our organization ensures maintenance of good relations with
subordinate [ ]

34 Superiors in our organization usually check mistakes and punish subordinates [ ]

35 My superiors give help and support [ ]

36 My superior listens to what I have to say [ ]

37. Superiors in our organization expect subordinates to do the job strictly [ ]
according to rules

38. The main purpose of supervision is to ensure achievement of targets [ ]

Conflict avoidance:

39. Conflicts are usually avoided and people prefer friendly atmosphere in TTD [ ]

40. Experts are consulted and their advice is sought in resolving conflicts [ ]

Warmth:

41. In TTD there is a relaxed and easy going working climate [ ]

42. There is a lot of warmth in the relationship between management and [ ]
employees in TTD

43. A friendly atmosphere prevails among the employees in TTD [ ]

Social Values:

44. TTD organization gives special attention to fulfill the social needs of the [ ] employees, in order to increase their social values

45. I am proud to be a member of TTD [ ]

46. The management of TTD encourages us to take part in social services [ ] and cultural programmes

47. I have high satisfaction that I am rendering social service to the society [ ] through TTD

Training and Advancement:

48. TTD provides adequate training programmes and facilities to its employees [ ]

49. Employees in TTD have many opportunities for their career advancement [ ]

50. TTD plans on regular basis for ensuring its employees career development [ ]

51. I have had sufficient job related training [ ]

Grievance Handling:

52. The TTD is always ready to handle the grievances and complaints of the employees [ ]

53. The grievance handling and settlement system existing in the TTD is effective [ ]

54. I am satisfied with the present system of grievance handling procedure in TTD[ ]

Individual Autonomy:

55. Employees are free to set their own performance goals in TTD [ ]

56. My work gives me opportunity of freedom and independence [ ]

Individual responsibility:

57. I always feel responsible at work [ ]

58. If at times things do not go well, I do take responsibility [ ]

Performance standards:

59. In TTD we set very high Standards for performance [ ]

60. There are rules and regulations for handling any kind of problem, which may [ ] arise in making most of the decisions

61. The goals that are set by the TTD are communicated to all the members to [ ] achieve them

62. The problems that are related to work are solved quickly [ ]

63. In TTD without any delay with regard to work [ ]

64. In TTD importance is given for high quality of work [ ]

Mutual trust:

65. Those who can achieve good results in the TTD organization are high trust [ ]

66. There is high trust between superiors and subordinates in the TTD organization [ ]

67. Employees in this organization really trust each other very much [ ]

68. Specialists and experts are highly trusted in TTD [ ]

Awards and rewards system:

69. Excellence in performance and getting tasks accomplished are highly rewarded in the TTD organization [ ]

70. Employees who keep up the tradition in this organization are duly recognized and rewarded [ ]

71. Team work in the TTD organization is encouraged and rewarded [ ]

72. Any thing goes wrong with the employees such employees are seriously reprimanded or punished [ ]

73. The management of TTD recognizes the efficiency of one's own work and accordingly employees are awarded [ ]

Work Relation:

74. The working relations between superiors and subordinates in TTD are cordial [ ]

75. The relations among the colleagues in our organization are healthy and friendly [ ]

76. Employees in TTD are very much concerned to help each other spontaneously [ ] when ever need arises

Decision making:

77. Decisions are made in consultation with the unions in TTD [ ]

78. Mainly the experts are involved in the decision making process [ ]

79. How often are you involved in decision making [ ]

Welfare facilities:

80. Medical facilities/ medical reimbursement provided by the employer are adequate [ ]

81. The Management of TTD provides adequate and qualitative educational services to the children of employees [ ]

82. TTD administration provides housing accommodation with water facilities [ ] at reasonable cost

203

83. I am convenient with the transport facilities from home to the work place   [   ]

84. TTD provides attractive retirement benefits to its employees   [   ]

85. The welfare facilities provided by TTD are far better than the welfare   [   ]
facilities provided by Govt.

Communication:

86. One way communication that is from top to bottom is in vogue in TTD   [   ]

87. Upward communication is accurate in our organization   [   ]

88. There is good communication across all sections in TTD   [   ]

89. Relevant information is available to all those who need and can use such   [   ]
information

90. Employees taking initiative in communicating concern for others   [   ]

91. Communication between subordinates and superiors is always open   [   ]

Unions:

92. TTD is not opposing the formation and functioning of the unions   [   ]

93. Trade union leadership is acquired on democratic lines in our organization   [   ]

94. There is no inter-union rivalry in this organization   [   ]

95. Issues for collective bargaining are determined with the consultation of   [   ]
union members

96. Unions in my organization are effective in solving the problems of the   [   ]
employees

97. Union-management relations are cordial   [   ]

Job Satisfaction:

Here under some aspects of Job content and Job context in TTD are given. Kindly express your level of Job satisfaction on a **five point scale** of opinion and select the appropriate one

    5- Highly Satisfied

    4- Satisfied

    3- Undecided

    2- Dissatisfied

    1- Highly Dissatisfied

Aspects of job	Level of satisfaction
98. Being an employee in TTD	[ ]
99. The present position in TTD	[ ]
100. Nature of job currently doing	[ ]

101. Salary being drawn on the current job   [   ]

102. Salary in relation to nature of job   [   ]

103. Salary in relation to experience on the job   [   ]

104. Salary in relation to educational qualification   [   ]

105. Salary that is being paid in TTD compared to the

     same cadre in other organizations   [   ]

106. Administrative policies of the TTD   [   ]

107. Superior-Subordinate relationship   [   ]

108. Working relationships among the colleagues   [   ]

109. Overall working condition in TTD   [   ]

110. The job status being enjoyed in TTD   [   ]

111. Work Achievement drive on the job being performed   [   ]

112. Authority and responsibility being enjoyed on the job   [   ]

113. Scope for future growth and development in life as an employee in TTD[   ]

114. Recognition being enjoyed in the society as an employee in TTD.   [   ]

115. Retirement benefits   [   ]

116. Transfer policy   [   ]

117. Promotional Avenues   [   ]

118. Kindly state any five factors that gave you the most satisfaction in TTD

Aspects of job

1.

2.

3.

4.

5.

Kindly also state any five factors that gave you the most dissatisfaction as an employee in TTD

1.

2.

3.

4.

5.   Signature of the Respondent/Employee

Thanking you Sir / Madam,

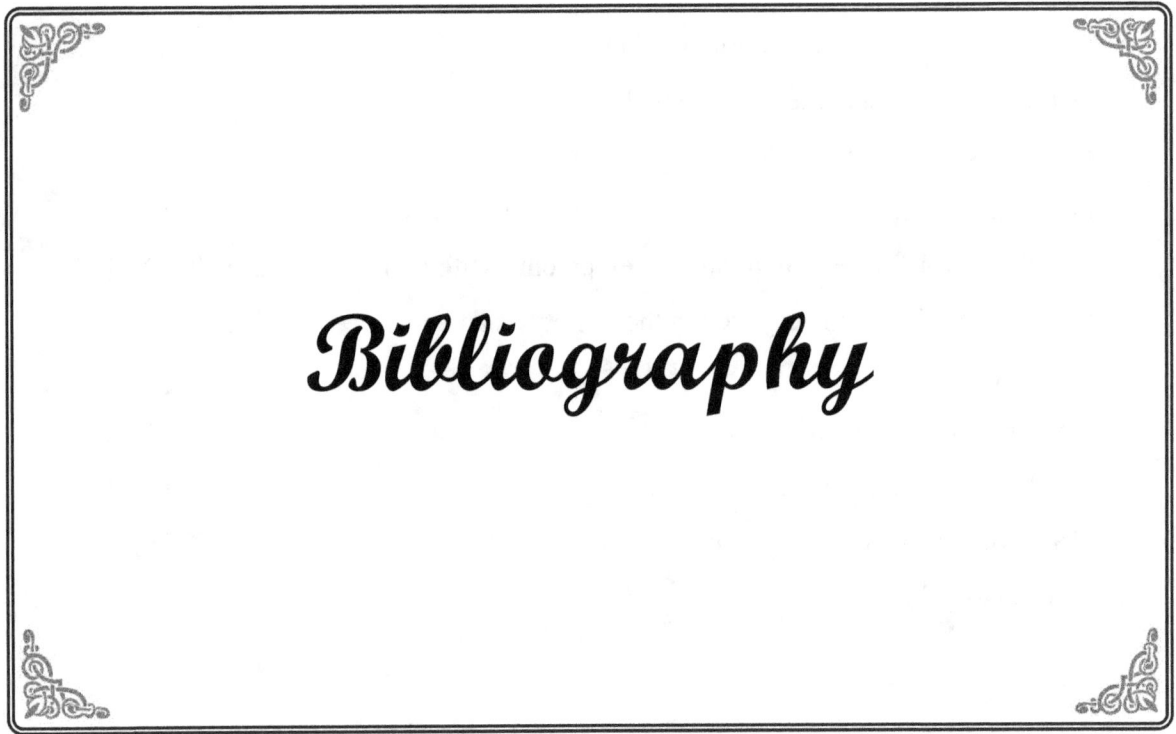

Bibliography

BOOKS

1. Baumgartel. H. 'The Perception of Modern Management Technology and Organisational Practices in Indian Business Organisation", Indian Administrative and Management Review, No.3, 1971, p.2.

2. Benjamin Schneider and Rover A. Snyder, "Some Relations Between Job Satisfaction and Organizational Climate, Journal of Applied Psychology, 60, No.3. 1975. p.318.

3. Bullock, R.P., "Social factors related to job satisfaction", Research Monograph, No. 70, Bureau of Business Research, Ohio State University, Columbus, 1952, p.92.

4. Campbell, J.P, Dunnette, M.D, Lawler, E.E, and Weick K.E. Jr "Managerial Behaviour, Performance and Effectiveness", New York: Mc Graw Hill, 1970, p.390.

5. Davis, K., "Human Behaviour at Work: Organisational Behaviour", (Sixth Edition), Tata MeGraw Hill Publishing Company Ltd., 1977, p.145.

6. Endowments Act No. 30 of 1987, Section 107 and Subsection (i)

7. Endowments Act No. 30 of 1987, Section 108 and Subsection (i)

8. Forehand,G.A., and B. Von H. Gilmer "Environmental Variations in Studies of Organisational Behaviour." Psychological Bulletin, Vol.62, No.6, December 1964, p.361-382.

9. Forehand,G.A., and B. Von H. Gilmer, op.cit, pp.361 -382.

10. Hanumantha Rao,B.S.L.,and Basaveswara Rao, "India History and Culture", Vol. III, Guntur: 1983, p.69.

11. Harrell, T.W., Industrial Psychology, Oxford Book Company, Calcutta, 1964.pp.34-54.

12. Herzberg, F., Mausner, B., and Synderman, B.B., "The Motivation to Work", New York, John Wiley, 1959, pp.2-99.

13. Hodgetts, Richhard M. "Organisational Behviour: Theory and Practice", Macmillan Publishing, 1991, pp.428-430.

14. Hoppock. R., "Job Satisfaction", Harper and Row, New York, 1935. p.42

15. Hoppock. R., op cit, p.42

16. James Francis,G and Gene Milbourn, Jr., Human Behaviour in the Work Environment: A Managerial Perspective, Goodyear Publishing Co., Santa Monica, California, 1980, p.92.

17. Joe Kelly, Organizational Behaviour, Richard D. Irwin, Inc, Illinois, 1980, p.483.

18. John E.Newman, "Development of a Measure of Perceived Work Environment", Academy of Management Journal, Vol.20, No.4, 1977, pp.520-534.

19. Kameswara Rao,V., Temples in and around Tirupati, 1986 p.5.

20. Korman, A.K., Organisational Behaviour, Prentice Hall of India, Private Ltd., New Delhi, 1978, p.18.

21. Krishnamurthy,P., Rayalaseemaloni Mukhya Devalayalu (in Telugu) Tirupati. 1982, p.37.

22. Krishnaswamy,T.,History of Tirumala Tirupati, TTD publications 1980, p. 138.

23. Lawrence R. James and Allan P. Jones, "Organisational Climate, A Review of Theory and Research," Psychological Bulletin, Vol. 81, Dec., 1974, p. 1098.

24. Likert, R.: The Human Organization. New York: McGraw Hill, 1967, P.113.

25. Litwin, G.H. and Stringer, R.A.: Motivation and Organisational Climate. Boston, Division of Research, Graduate School of Business Administration, Harvard University, 1968, pp.213-215.

26. Op. cit, p.391.

27. Locke, Job satisfaction. In M. Gruenberg and Y. Wall (eds) Social psychology and organizational behaviour; (London: Wiley), 1984, pp.22-28.

28. Luthans, F., Organizational Behaviour (Fifth Edition), McGraw Hill Series in Management, 1989, pp.82-89.

29. Maslow, A.H., A Theory of Human Motivation", Psychological Review", Vol.50, 1943, pp. 370-396.

30. Mumford, E., job Satisfaction – A Study of Computer Specialists, Longman, 1972, p.82.

31. Pareek, U., Motivational Analysis of Organization's Climate in Developing Human Resources, Annual, 1987, University Association, San Diego, pp. 160-180.

32. Pestonjee, D.M., "Motivation and Job Satisfaction", McMillan India Ltd., New Delhi, 1991.

33. Op.cit, p.42

34. Pritchard Robert D., and Bernard W. Karasick. "The Effects of Orgnisational Climate on Managerial Job performance and Job Satisfaction," Organisational Behaviour and Human Performance, Vol.9. 1973. pp. 126-146.

35. Op cit., p.24

36. Roeth Lirsberger, F.J. and Diskson, W.J., Management and the Worker, Harvard University Press, Cambridge, 1939.

37. Schneider, B., and C.J. Bartlett, "Individual differences and Organisational Climate." Personnel Psychology, No. 21, 1968, pp. 323-334.

38. Scott, T.B., Davis, R.V., England, G.W. and Lofquist, L.H., A Definition of Work Adjustment, Minnesota Studies in Vocational Rehabilitation: Industrial Relations Centre, University of Minnesota, Minnesota, 1960.

39. Siegel, L., Industrial Psychology, Irwin, Homewood, 1962.

40. Sitapathi,P., "Art and Sculpture in Sri Venkateswara Swamy temple", T.T.D Tirupati, 1986, p. 24.

41. Sitapathi,P., Sri Venkateswara, the Lord of the Seven Hills Tirupati: Bharatiya Vidya Bhavan, 1977, p.86.

42. Smith H.C., "Psychology of Industrial Behaviour", McGraw Hill, New York, 1955. p.46

43. Surya Kumar Srivastava "Relationship Between Job Satisfaction and Organizational Climate" Published Book, Print well Publishers, Jaipur (India) 1990.

44. T.T.D. Administration Report 1998-99 pp.1-5.

45. Op.cit. p. 392.

46. The word "Vengadam" is considered the holiest hill of Vishnu Kshetrams in India, i.e. Tirumala hills.

47. Veeraraghavachary, T.K.T, "History of Tirupati", T.T.D. Vol.1, 1953, p.10.

48. Vroom, V.H., "Work and Motivation", New York, John Wiley and sons, 1964.

ARTICLES FROM JOURNALS

1. Akhyilesh, K.B., and Pondey, S., "A Comparative Study of Organizational Climate in Two Banks", Indian Journal of Industrial Relations, Vol.21, No.4, April 1986, pp.456-461.

2. Antony Joseph "Job Ssatisfaction Among Transport Employees", Journal of Psychological Researches, Vol.45, No.2, 2001, pp.58-61.

3. Archana Tarabadkar and Rehana Ghadially "Achievement Motivation and Job Satisfaction", Productivity, Vol. XXVI, No.3 1985, pp.231-237.

4. Arya, P.P., "Work Satisfaction and its Correlates", Indian Journal of Industrial Relations, Vol. 20, No. 1, July 1984, pp. 89-100.

5. Avinash Kumar Srivastav "Achievement Climate in Public Sector – A Cross Functional Study on Relationship with Stress and Coping" IIMB Management Review, Vol.19, No.4, December 2007, pp.415-425.

6. Avinash Kumar Srivastav, "Organizational Climate in Public Sector: An Empirical Study", Management & Change Vol.10, No.2, 2006, pp.65-76.

7. Bahadur katuwal and Gurprect Randhawa " Study of Job Satisfaction of Public and Private Sector Nepalese Textile Workers" Indian Journal of Industrial Relations Vol.43, No.23, October 2007, pp.239-253.

8. Bhowon, U., and Ah-kion, J., "Organizational Climate and Stress- A study of Managers in Mauritius", Psychological Studies, Vol. 49, No. 1, January 2004, pp. 45-51.

9. Bose, S., and Agarwal, M., "Organizational Work Climate and Perceived 'Procedural Fairness' of Human Resource Practices", Psychological Studies, Vol. 50, No. 2, and 3, April and July 2005, pp. 243- 249

10. Carrell, M.R., Elbert, N.F., "Some Personal and Organisational Determinants of Job Satisfaction of Postal Clerks", Academy of Management Journal, Vol. 17, No. 2, June 1974, pp. 368 – 372.

11. Chatterji, R., "Job Satisfaction", Industrial Relations, Vol. 12, 1960, pp. 262-264.

12. Dhillion, P.K., "Moderate Effects on the Occupational Stress –Job Satisfaction Relationship", Productivity, Vol. 31, No. 4, January – March, 1991, pp.584-590.

13. Dolke, A.M., "Personal – Personality, Job and Organisational Correlates of Work Identification", The Indian Journal of Social Work, Vol. LII, No. 4, Oct 1991, pp. 621-633.

14. Downey, H.K., Hellricgel, D., and Slocum, J.W., "Congruence Between Individual Needs, Organisational Climate, Job Satisfaction and Performance", Academy of Management Journal, Vol. 18, No. 1, March 1975, pp. 149-155.

15. Dwivedi, R.S., "Anatomy of Organizational Climate ", Journal of the All India Management Association, Vol. 18, No. 5, May 1979, pp.25-28, 36.

16. Ewen, R.B., "Some Determinants of Job Satisfaction: A Study of the Generality of Herzberg's Theory", Journal of Applied Psychology, Vol.48, N0.3, 1964, pp161-163.

17. Frank Friedlander "Job Characteristics as Satisfiers and Dissatisfiers", Journal of Applied Psychology, Vol.48, N0.6, 1964 pp.388-392.

18. Frederisken N, "Some Effects of Organisational Climate on Administrative Performance,Research Memorandum, 1966 p-401.

19. Gani, A., and Farooq A. Sash., "Correlates of Organisational Climate in Banking Industry", Indian Journal of Industrial Relations, Vol.36, No.3, January 2001, pp. 301-322.

20. Giri, V.N., and Pavan Kumar, B., "Impact of Organisational Climate on Job Satisfaction and Job Performance", National Academy of Psychology, India, Vol. 52, No.2, 2007, pp. 131-133.

21. Guha T.N "Job Satisfaction Among Shoe Factory Workers", Productivity, Vol.VI, No.1, 1965 pp89-94.

22. Hellriegel, D., and Slocum, J.W., "Organizational Climate: Measures, Research and Contingencies", Academy of Management Journal, Vol. 17, No. 2, June 1974, pp. 255-280.

23. Jahan, R. and Haque, S., "Effects of Organisational Climate on Job Involvement, Job Satisfaction and Personality of Mid – level Managers", The Bangladesh Journal of Psychology, 1993, pp. 35-42.

24. Klaleque, A., and Choudhury, N.,"Job Facets and Overall Job Satisfaction of Industrial Managers", Indian Journal of Industrial Relations, Vol. 20, No. 1, July 1984, pp. 55-64

25. Lawler, E.E., Hall, D.T., and Oldham, G.R., "Organizational Climate: Relationship to Organizational Structure, Process and Performance", Organizational Behaviour and Human Performance, Vol. 11, No.1 Feb 1974, pp. 139-155.

26. Lyon H.L., and Ivancevich J.M., "An Exploratory Investigation of Organizational Climate and Job Satisfaction in a Hospital" Academy of Management Journal Vol.17, No.4, 1974 pp.635-648.

27. Malik, K., and Goyal, D.P., "Organizational Environment and Information System", Vikalpa, Vol. 28, No. 1, January- March 2003, pp.61-74.

28. Muchinsky, P.M., "Organisational Communication: Relationship to Organisational Climate and Job Satisfaction", Academy of Management Journal, Vol. 20, No. 4, 1977,pp. 592-607.

29. Nataraj, C.L., and Hafeez, A., "A Study of Job Satisfaction Among Skilled Workers", The Indian Journal of Social Work, Vol. XXVI, No. 1, April 1965, pp. 9-12.

30. Natarajan, R., "A Study on Organizational Climate and Teacher Morale", Journal of Psychological Researches, Vol. 45, No. 1, 2001, pp. 19 – 2 1.

31. Offeremann, L.R., and Malamut, A.B., "When Leaders Harass: The Impact of Target Perceptions of Organizational Leadership and Climate on Harassment Reporting and Outcomes", Journal of Applied Psychology, Vol.87, No. 5, pp. 885-893.

32. Pallavi Shash, "Need Importance and Need Fulfillment in Management Levels", Indian Management, May 1976, pp. 29-31, 45,

33. Payne, R.L., Fineman, S., and Wall, T.D., "Organisational Climate and Job Satisfaction: A Conceptual Synthesis", Organisational Behaviour and Human Performance, Vol. 16, No. 1, June 1976, pp. 45-62.

34. Peterson, R.B., "The Interaction of Technological Process Organizational Climate in Norwegian Firms", Academy of Management Journal, Vol. 18, June 1975, pp.288-299.

35. Poonam Bajaj., "Alienation as Related to Perception of Organizational Climate", Indian Journal of Industrial Relations, Vol. 17. No. 4, April 1982, pp.563-572.

36. Pramod Kumar, and Chandrakala Bora, "Job Satisfaction and Perceived Organisational Climate ", The Indian Journal of Social Work, Vol. XL, No. 1, April 1979. pp. 23-26.

37. Pritchard R.D., and Karasick B.W., "The Effects of Organizational Climate on Managerial Job Performance and Job Satisfaction", Organizational Behaviour and Human Performance, Vol.9, No.1, February, 1973 pp.126-146.

38. Sanjay Kumar Singh, " Organizational Climate and Role Stress as Correlates of Journalistic Writing Attitude", Indian Journal of Industrial Relations, Vol. 41, No. 2, October 2005, pp. 206- 217.

39. Sarveswara Rao, G.V., and Ganapathi Rao, V., "A Study of Factors Contributing to Satisfaction and Importance of Industrial Personnel : A Test of the Two Factory Theory", Indian Journal of Industrial Relations, Vol. 9, No. 2, Oct 1973, pp. 233-262.

214

40. Sayeed, O.B., "Organisational Effectiveness: Relationship with Job Satisfaction Facets", Productivity, Vol. 33, No. 3, October- December, 1992. pp. 422-429

41. Schneider, B., "Organisational Climate: An Essay", Personal Psychology, Vol. 28, No. 4, winter 1975, pp. 447-479.

42. Schneider, B., and Snyder, R.A., "Some Relationship between Job Satisfaction and Organisational Climate", Journal of Applied Psychology, Vol. 60, No. 3, June 1975, pp. 318-328.

43. Sebastian, M.P., and Bhargava, S., "Organizational Climate of Non- Profit Organization", Productivity, Vol. 43, No. 4, January-March, 2003, pp. 611-618.

44. Sharma R.D., and Jeevan Jyoti "Job Satisfaction Among School Teachers", IIMB Management Review, Vol.18, No.4 December, 2006 pp.349-363.

45. Sharma, B.R., "Employee Motivation and Employer –Employee Relations In India", Indian Management, June 1983 pp. 8-14.

46. Sharma, B.R., and Venkata Ratnam, C.S., "Organizational Climate and Supervisory – Management Relations in Ispat Nigam", Indian Journal of Industrial Relations, Vol. 23, No. 1, July, 1987. pp. 1-28.

47. Sharma, V.c., Gaur, A.K., Srivastava, S.K., and Pandey, R.S., "Job Satisfaction of Women Workers", The Indian Journal of Commerce, Vol.54, No.4, Oct.-Dec. 2001, pp. 157-163.

48. Sing, A.P., and Sadhana Singh "Effects of Stress and Work Culture on Job Satisfaction" The Icfai University Journal of Organizational Behaviour, Vol. VIII, No.2, Aprial 2009, pp- 52-62

49. Singh, S.P., and Singh, A.P., "The Effect of Certain and Personal Factors on Job Satisfaction of Supervisors", Psychological Studies, Vol.25, 1961, pp. 127-132.

50. Sinha and Sharma "Union Attitude and Job Satisfaction in Indian workers". Journal of Applied Psychology, Vol.46, No.4, 1962, pp.247-251.

51. Sinha, B.P., and Gupta, p., et.al "Societal Beliefs, Organizational Climate, and Managers' Self- Perceptions", Vikalpa, Vol. 26, No. 1, January-March 2001, pp. 33-47.

52. Srimannarayana. M., "Human Resource Development Climate in Dubai Organizations" Indian Journal of Industrial Relations, Vol. 43, No.1, July 2007, pp. 1-12.

53. Srivastava, A.K., "Motivation and Perception of Organizational Climate" Productivity, Vol. XXXVI, N.1, 1985, pp.55-58.

54. Sumanlata," A Study of Educational Attainment as Function of School Organizational Climate", Educational Research in Education and Psychology, Vol. 10, No. 3, 4, 2005, pp. 100-103 .

55. Sushila Singhal, "Measurement of Job Satisfaction on a Three – Dimensional Plane", Indian Journal of Industrial Relations, Vol. 9, No. 2, Oct 1973, pp. 263-279.

56. Taylor. H, "The Differences between Exercisers and Non-exercisers on Work Related Variables", International Journal of Stress Management, Vol. 7, 2000, pp.307-309.

57. Uma Bhowon., "Perceived Organisational Climate and Interpersonal Conflict Handling Strategies", Indian Journal of Industrial Relations, Vol.35, No.1, July 1999, pp. 43-54.

58. Wallace, J.R., Ivancevich, J.M., And Lyon, H.L., "Measurement Modification for Assessing Organizational Climate in Hospitals", Academy of Management Journal, Vol. 18, No.1 March 1975, pp. 82 97.

THESES

1. Bhagavan,S.G.S., Finances of the TTD Educational Institutions, unpublished thesis submitted to S.V.University, Tirupati, 1995 pp.38, 39.

2. Chakrapani, D., "Job Satisfaction Among Employees of Select Manufacturing Units in Cuddapah, Andhra Pradesh", Unpublished Ph.D. thesis in Commerce, submitted to S.V.University, Tirupati. 2001.

3. Rama Devi, V., "Faculty Job Satisfaction and their views on Management – Study of two Universities in Andhra Pradesh" unpublished Ph.D. thesis in Commerce, submitted to S.K.University, Anantapur.

4. Sailaja Rani "Job Satisfaction Among Bank Employees in Chittoor District of A.P." Thesis Submitted to S.V University, Tirupati, March 2006.

5. Subramanyam,J., "Personnel Management in T.T.D." unpublished thesis submitted to S.V.University, Tirupati, 1987 pp.36, 37.

6. Venkatarathnam Achari, K.P., Tirumala Tirupati – A Study in Religion and Society, unpublished thesis submitted to S.V.University, Tirupati, 1992 p.60.

7. Vivekananda Reddy. "The Educational Administration in TTD – A Study" Unpublished thesis submitted to S.V.University, Tirupati, 1995 p.62 .